BLIMEY, I'M KNACKERED!

IMBRIFEX
BOOKS

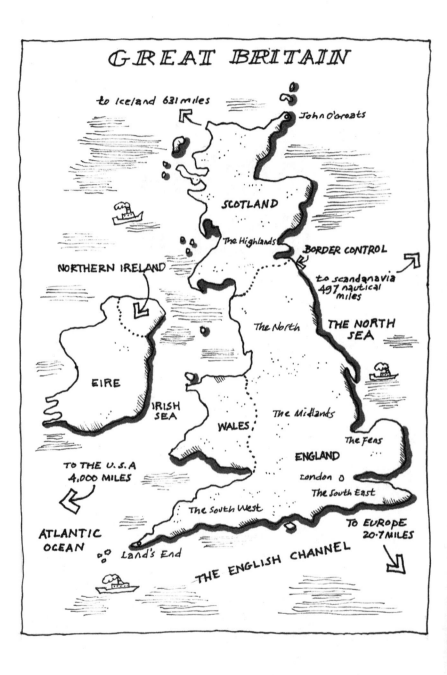

BLIMEY, I'M KNACKERED!

An American's Survival
Guide to British English

MARSHALL HALL

IMBRIFEX BOOKS

IMBRIFEX BOOKS
8275 S. Eastern Avenue, Suite 200
Las Vegas, NV 89123
Imbrifex.com

This publication is provided for informational, educational, and entertainment purposes. The information contained in this publication is true to the best of our knowledge. Corrections, updated and suggestions may be sent to the author at: books@imbrifex.com.

Editors: Peter Thody, David Johnstone, Tom Herbertson
Illustrator: Mark Cowie
Cover and Book Designer: Sue Campbell Book Design
Author Photo: Peter Thody

Library of Congress Cataloging-in-Publication Data

Names: Hall, Marshall, 1951- author.
Title: Blimey, I'm knackered! : an American's survival guide to British English / Marshall Hall.
Description: First edition. | Las Vegas : Imbrifex Books, 2021. | Includes index. | Summary: "Blimey, I'm Knackered is the perfect companion for anyone desiring to bridge the gap between US and UK English or who simply enjoys the evolution of language and culture. American scholar and longtime UK resident Marshall Hall has organized his insightful definitions and explanations of British idioms, colloquialisms, abbreviations, acronyms, and slang into nineteen entertaining and revealing chapters covering everything from transportation and food to politics, education, and wardrobe"-- Provided by publisher.
Identifiers: LCCN 2020054254 (print) | LCCN 2020054255 (ebook) | ISBN 9781945501494 (hardcover) | ISBN 9781945501500 (epub)
Subjects: LCSH: English language--Great Britain--Glossaries, vocabularies, etc. | English language--Great Britain--Terms and phrases.
Classification: LCC PE1704 .H35 2021 (print) | LCC PE1704 (ebook) | DDC 427/.941--dc23
LC record available at https://lccn.loc.gov/2020054254
LC ebook record available at https://lccn.loc.gov/2020054255

First Edition: August 2021
Printed in the United States of America

IMBRIFEX® is registered trademark of Flattop Productions, Inc.

Dedicated to my daughters
Anne, Katie, and Sarah

Contents

"England and America are two countries
separated by a common language."

—George Bernard Shaw

Introduction

THE ENGLISH LANGUAGE IS A MALLEABLE AND YET TENACIOUS thing. It has an amazing number of manifestations in every continent on the globe. It allows for adaptations, additions, omissions, and local variations, and still, or perhaps because of it, offers one of the greatest media for personal expression in human history.

British English and American English are no exceptions to this generic and individual growth phenomenon, and each has evolved along separate lines of influence for well over three hundred years. The resulting differences mean that travelers arriving in the UK for the first time are confronted by a bewildering collection of words, spellings, colloquialisms, and pronunciations, all wonderful parts of what they had previously thought was the same language. Even with increasing world travel and corporate globalization, regional English pride and stubbornness ensure that British English remains particularly rich with local expressions and pronunciations. These continue to be some of the primary fascinations Americans have with England and the rest of the United Kingdom.

This book was written by an American living in Britain for the assistance of fellow Americans planning to visit this great country and for the amusement of our British friends. It started at a party one evening as a humorous list of the idiosyncrasies of British English compared to American English. Every American expat has accumulated stories of how they or a friend have been embarrassed by some naive misuse of British English. Many of those stories are included here. We started to list the differences, and in a matter of minutes had more than a hundred. Over the ensuing weeks as friends, family, and colleagues heard of the list, e-mails started to arrive with contributions and tales. Every evening out, every dinner conversation, and every casual greeting at the university generated an additional few entries. The fun list soon turned into a group project with nearly seven hundred identified differences.

Once the list had been compiled, the challenge became one of definition. We soon discovered that there are no written, institutionalized, or even commonly accepted definitions for most of the entries. Meanings in one part of Britain had evolved to become something different in another part, and many wine-soaked discussions erupted over what certain things meant locally. The task was eventually organized into nineteen categories, as reflected in the table of contents. Many entries fell into several sections, and decisions had to be made as to where they fit the best. The colloquialisms were undoubtedly the sources of the most humor and discussion.

Over the subsequent months, the definitions—and sometimes pronunciations—were written, researched, debated, and rewritten. As new entries arrived, everyone involved in the project began to realize that our list was not definitive. There are unquestionably hundreds of variations and new words that have been overlooked or we have yet to hear. More poignantly, though, we recognized that the very thing we find so interesting about the English language—its ability to grow and change into new forms—means that this collection of definitions and humorous anecdotes has a finite lifespan.

1.

Buildings and Structures

THE ARCHITECTURE OF THE UK IS THE RESULT OF A MULTITUDE of influences, including cultural values, expediency, local building materials, urban density, and available expertise. Visitors to Edinburgh, as an example, will no doubt notice architectural styles, building materials, and urban layouts that are distinctly different from the red brick and Portland stone of London. The countryside has its own historic and often very practical styles that include thatched roofs that are newly installed and maintained even today.

The population booms of the Victorian and post-World War II eras called for new ways of thinking about and constructing housing for the masses. In the late nineteenth century, this resulted in excessively long terraces of houses sharing common dividing walls with "two up-two down" room layouts and an outdoor toilet. From the 1950s to the 1970s, the Victorian terraced houses were seen as slums, and many were cleared away to make room for the new and modern high-rise tower blocks, which have themselves started to be cleared away for the next wave of high-density housing. Both have enjoyed a regeneration in recent decades as demonstrated by the protective historical listing given to several of the high-rise tower blocks and seen in the gentrification of the London Docklands and other London, Manchester, Glasgow, and many other city neighborhoods.

For practical reasons, houses in the UK are not built of wood. It's just too damp, and clay tiles are the roofing material of almost all housing. Residential interiors also reflect a unique value and class system that Americans might find it difficult to understand. In many rural communities, toilets only started moving indoors in the last hundred years, central heating is a modern luxury, and mixer valves for the baths and sinks are still sometimes difficult to find.

BACK-TO-BACK HOUSE

A back-to-back shares three walls with other properties (the back wall and both sides), so the door and windows are on the front of the house. The typical back-to-back house had a living room and kitchen on the ground floor, a bedroom on the first and attic floors, plus a basement. It was renowned for squalor, disease, and poverty due to the cramped design and poor sanitation. In the eighteenth and nineteenth centuries, mill and mine owners of the Midlands and northern England built mile upon mile of them to cram the maximum number of workers into the minimum space at the lowest possible cost. Few back-to-back houses have survived besides some in the West Yorkshire cities of Leeds and Bradford. Elsewhere, the National Trust has saved a small number, including six in Birmingham out of the original sixty thousand in that city.

BLOCK OF FLATS
An apartment building.

BREEZEBLOCK
Cinderblock.

BUNGALOW
A smallish (by American standards) single-story fully detached house. The word is derived from the Hindustani word "bangala," meaning "belonging to Bengal," in reference to the type of houses built by early European settlers. (The folk etymology that claims the word is derived from "build four short walls, and 'bung a low' roof on it" is unsubstantiated.) The bungalow became popular as an architectural style in the late nineteenth century.

BUREAU-DE-CHANGE
A currency exchange.

COAL HOLE
An interesting bit of history. As you walk along the streets of any large English city, look down at the sidewalk (pavement), and you will see small steel discs approximately fifteen inches in diameter. They cover holes through which the coal merchant could deliver coal to the basement of a townhouse without needing entry. These holes were

known as "coal holes." Some older coal hole covers are quite intricate and collectible, while many of the modern ones are just plain. Coal holes were rendered obsolete in the 1950s with the introduction of gas heating systems and legislation requiring smokeless fuel.

COUNCIL HOUSE

A residential property owned by the local council that people who meet specific low-income criteria can rent for comparatively low rates. Every council in the UK has these. A large collection of these is known as a "council estate." Similar types of government-subsidized property in the USA are sometimes known as "projects." In the USA, an apartment in a project is always a rental property, but in the UK, public-sector tenants have the option to purchase council houses. Because of this, the available stock of rental properties is rapidly decreasing. See **Council** page 281.

DES RES

A real estate agent term, short for "desirable residence."

DETACHED HOUSE

A house that sits on its own piece of ground without other houses attached to either side. While this is common in America, the relatively high value of land in the UK makes this type of property less widely affordable.

DPC

Damp proof course. A layer of waterproof membrane laid into the brickwork a few inches above the ground to prevent the transfer of moisture up the brick wall.

END-OF-TERRACE HOUSE

See **Terraced house** page 21.

ENGLISH HERITAGE

A charitable organization formed in 1983 that manages historic buildings and ancient monuments in England, such as the stone circles, great castles and abbeys, historic houses, and other unique sites.

FIRST FLOOR

The floor above ground level. In the USA, this is called the "second floor."

FREEHOLD

Outright ownership of a house or flat without any associated owners such as a landlord. This is compared to a leasehold, which is sold for a fixed period of time, e.g., ninety-nine years, and which reverts back to the landlord freeholder at the end of the leasehold.

GAZUMP

A technique used by property speculators who offer a higher offer to purchase a property beyond what the seller and another would-be purchaser have agreed to. "Buyers have no rights whatsoever if they find themselves gazumped before a contract has been signed." (This word is related to "gazunder," whereby a buyer reduces the agreed-to price prior to execution of the sale contract.)

GAOL

A Gaelic word for jail or prison (pronounced "jail"). Used in Northern Ireland and Scotland. In the United Kingdom, "jail" and "prison" are interchangeable terms, and their meanings are different from those in the USA.

GRANNY FLAT

A renovation or addition to a residence, ostensibly to house an elderly relative. In the USA, they're often referred to as "mother-in-law apartments."

GROUND FLOOR

The floor of a building at ground level. In the USA, this is usually called the "first floor."

HOARDINGS

Pieces of plywood, plastic-covered scaffolding, or corrugated steel that hide a construction site. Also, a large board used for displaying advertising posters by a road. Americans call these "billboards." The term is also applied to the ground-level panels that carry advertising messages on the sides of the playing fields at sports stadiums.

HOUSING ESTATE

A subdivision with many dwellings. Usually confined to urban areas, these have become the blight of English architecture and the origin of much social unrest.

INDUSTRIAL ESTATE

An area containing an aggregation of small manufacturing companies, offices, and service providers, usually located on the edge of a town. In recent years, industrial estates may have become specialized in specific functions such as automobiles, DIY services, or wholesale restaurant supply.

IRONMONGER

Historically, a person or store that deals in iron and hardware. The American term is "hardware store."

LEASEHOLD

Ownership of a flat or house, which is sold for a fixed period of time and reverts back to the landlord freeholder at the end of the leasehold.

LIFT

An elevator.

LOFT

The term "loft" is virtually interchangeable with attic, but Brits are more likely to refer to "loft conversions" and "loft apartments." Unlike attics, lofts in the USA are often not enclosed. In addition, the term has recently been expanded to mean a variety of both residential and commercial spaces.

MAINS POWER

240 volts of electricity supplied to a building via the public network. Be careful NOT to plug an American (110 volt) hairdryer or other electrical appliance into an outlet without using a converter!

MAINS WATER

The fresh water supplied to a building through pipes connected to the community water supply system.

MAISONETTE

A two-story apartment with its own outside entrance. The name derives from the French term for "small house" and is most analogous to a townhouse in the USA.

MEWS

A street or small area that was built in the eighteenth or nineteenth century and was used in the past for keeping horses but is now used as a house. Today, many mews houses have been tastefully restored to provide everything required for a chic and enjoyable twenty-first-century lifestyle.

MID-TERRACE HOUSE

See **Terraced house** page 21.

Mid-Terrace House

MOD CONS

A modern real estate agent term referring to "modern conveniences" (e.g., central heating, air conditioning, mixer valves) in houses and apartments. The term shows up in real estate advertisements in phrases such as "All mod cons."

MUSIC HALL

A theater or auditorium for popular entertainment in the nineteenth and early twentieth centuries. Known for variety shows featuring six to eight performances by singers, musicians, comedians, dances, and feats of physical prowess. At the turn of the century, there were hundreds of these across England. In London, the Windmill Theatre on Windmill Street—famous for never closing during WWII—is one of the best-known. In the USA, the analogous entertainment form is called "vaudeville."

PARADE OF SHOPS

Also widely referred to as a "shopping parade," this is a row of assorted stores (e.g., newsstand, butcher, grocer, fast food outlet, bookie, thrift store), usually in a residential part of town. If someone says, "I'm off to the shops," it's safe to assume they mean the local parade. This is different from a "strip mall" in the USA. What Americans call a "strip mall" is known as a "retail outlet" in the UK.

PERSPEX

Plexiglas.

PLASTERBOARD

Drywall.

SEMI-DETACHED HOUSE

A house with one side attached to another house, known in the USA as a "duplex."

SHOP FRONT

A storefront, a window of a store or shop facing the street used to display merchandise.

STATIONERS

A shop that specializes in office supplies, including stationery.

TERRACED HOUSE

During the building boom of the early Victorian age, hundreds of thousands of these rows of houses were built across Britain to provide affordable housing for the populace, most of whom were factory or mine workers supporting the industrial revolution. As many as fifty to sixty of these houses shared common walls on both sides, had a small garden in the rear, and had communal passageways to the rear of the properties. A house in the middle of one of these rows is known as a "mid-terrace house," and one on the end is known as an "end-of-terrace house." See **Back-to-back house** page 12.

TO LET

To rent a property to another person. Often seen on signs.

TOWER BLOCK

High-rise housing built by the government in post-war Britain, usually found in housing estates. These were widely seen as mass housing for the poor, often replacing rundown terraced houses. Many have since been demolished and replaced by low- or mid-rise apartments, but recent years have seen a huge resurgence in the building of "tall towers" for middle-class

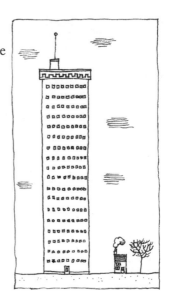

21

city-center dwellers. They also provide good-quality, high-density accommodation for college students. One comparable term in the USA would be "mid- to high-rise apartment buildings."

TWO UP-TWO DOWN

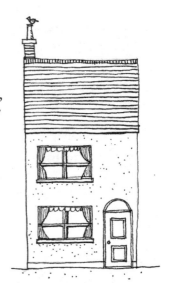

A term describing the room arrangement of a terraced house in industrial Britain, usually consisting of a kitchen/ dining room and a living room on the ground floor and two bedrooms upstairs. The toilet was usually detached from the house and was therefore known as the "outhouse." See **Terraced house** page 21.

YARD

A surface paved with concrete, brick, stone, or other material. Not grassy and often not residential. As in the USA, it is becoming common for Britons to refer to "backyards," which might have grass or other gardens in them. See **Garden** page 191.

2.

Colloquialisms

A COLLOQUIALISM IS AN INFORMAL EXPRESSION USED IN vernacular speech, and these are what will convince the visitor to the UK that we do actually speak two different languages. They are simultaneously fascinating and baffling and the cause of constant wonder about their origin. "Where did that come from?" The word "colloquialism" comes from Latin and means a conversation. As a linguistic device, it refers to the use of informal or everyday language. Colloquialisms are generally regional, in that they often belong to a certain area or local dialect. They can be words or phrases. Native speakers of a language understand and use colloquialisms without realizing it, while non-native speakers may find colloquial expressions hard to understand and translate. This is because many colloquialisms do not use words literally but instead use them idiomatically or metaphorically. Get ready, because a lot of them could make you laugh out loud.

ALL FUR COAT AND NO KNICKERS

Referring to a woman who looks good on the surface but has no substance.

ARGY-BARGY

A big deal, usually an emotional crisis, a lively discussion or dispute, an argument or quarrel. "There was a bit of argy-bargy between the two of them, but they shook hands later." Some argue that "argy" is a modification of the word "argue."

AT HER MAJESTY'S PLEASURE

Being locked up in prison for life.

AT THE END OF THE DAY

An idiom meaning "The final result will be." It may also imply that there's not a lot we can do about it anyway. When all's said and done, this will happen anyway. Also heard quite a bit in the USA these days, but the UK claims first use.

> "I love England because it's like a grown-up America, a fact I'm reminded of as soon as I get on a British Airways flight or hop into a London cab and people stop treating me as though I'd just learned to finger paint."
>
> —Chuck Thompson

BALL AND CHAIN

A wife or female spouse. Referring to the ball and chain attached to the ankles of prisoners in times gone by.

BEE'S KNEES

The most excellent, the best. See **Cat's Whiskers** page 60.

BEGGAR OFF

Meaning "Go away," an old-fashioned term that originated from evicting someone from your house and effectively telling them to go and beg. Could also be a more courteous version of "Bugger off." See **Bugger off** page 60.

BELT AND BRACES

Reference to a belt and suspenders, meaning to double-ensure something or to add redundancy.

BET YOUR BOLLOCKS

Slang for a indicating a certainty.

BET YOUR BOOTS

Slang for indicating a certainty.

BETTER THAN A POKE IN THE EYE WITH A BLUNT STICK

Used to express that the situation could have been worse.

BETTER THAN A SMACK IN THE FACE WITH A WET HALIBUT

As with "Better than a poke in the eye with a blunt stick," this is a phrase used to indicate that things aren't quite as bad as a they might be. Variations include wet kipper, wet trout, and the generic wet fish. A 1971 Monty Python sketch called "The Fish-Slapping Dance" may have encouraged the use of this phrase.

BIT OF CRUMPET

A woman when viewed as a sex object or potential sexual partner.

BOB'S YOUR UNCLE

A colloquialism meaning "And there you have it" or "Job done." "All I need to do now is reconnect those wires, and Bob's your uncle." There are various explanations as to where the expression originated—none certain—but perhaps the most plausible stems from the appointment of one Arthur Balfour to various political posts in the 1880s (for which he was eminently underqualified) by his uncle Robert Arthur Talbot Gascoyne-Cecil, 3rd Marquess of Salisbury. "It's all sorted, Bob's your uncle."

CAT AMONG THE PIGEONS

To say something or release an agent that causes major upset or disruption. (For example, "I accidently let her secret out, and that's really put the cat among the pigeons.")

CHALK AND CHEESE

A remark indicating that two things, usually people, are very different from one another. For example, "Those two are like chalk and cheese, they are."

CHEERS

Expressing good wishes with a drink. Traditionally, glasses are knocked together while "Cheers" is exclaimed and a drink is taken. "Cheers" can also be used generally to replace "Thanks" and as a sign-off from a conversation.

COCK A SNOOK

To regard someone or something with disrespect or to express defiance. To "cock a snook" is to spread a hand with the thumb on the nose, preferably with crossed eyes, waggling fingers, and any other annoying gesticulation that comes to mind at the time. It's what Americans call "thumbing their nose at someone."

COME A CROPPER

To suffer a misfortune, to fall, to have an accident.

COMMON AS MUCK

A derogatory term applied to a person considered "a bit rough" or vulgar. Someone who speaks or acts very badly.

CRACK ON

To get on with something or continue doing something.

DEL BOY

A person who is a bit of a deal maker or "wheeler dealer," always on the lookout for an opportunity to make money. Derived from Derek Trotter, a character in the TV series *Only Fools and Horses*, played by David Jason.

DO A RUNNER

To run away from responsibilities or commitments, especially ones that will attract the attention of the police, e.g., a restaurant bill or a car crash.

DOG'S BOLLOCKS

The very best, often abbreviated to just "Dog's." "My new car is the absolute dog's." See **Cat's Whiskers** page 60.

DOG'S DINNER

An expression describing a mess or something that has been bungled." Confusingly, it may also be used as a back-handed compliment for someone whose dress is overly flashy and ostentatious. "Where are you going dressed like a dog's dinner?" "Dog's breakfast" is another term used to describe a mess or a job done badly.

DOING PORRIDGE

An idiom for spending time in prison. For many years in British jails, porridge, (oatmeal) was the only breakfast choice. Interestingly, porridge has now been removed from British prison menus. Not only was it being used—presumably once it had set—to block up door locks, the oats could also be used to brew illicit hooch.

DOLE

Welfare payments given to the unemployed. If someone is receiving these benefits, they are said to be "On the dole."

DOOLALLY-TAP

To say someone is "doolally-tap" means that they are mad, or at least very eccentric. The phrase comes from Deolali, the name of a former British army camp 100 miles northeast of Bombay, used as a transit station and sanitarium for soldiers awaiting transport back to Britain. Some say that it means malarial fever or swamp fever.

DRIVE ME AROUND THE BEND

Drive me crazy.

DROP A CLANGER

To make a mistake, particularly a *faux pas*.

EXCUSE ME

Omnipresent in England's vocabulary, this phrase is used for all manner of verbal expression. It seems to be heard much more than in American English. Uses include:
   – Asking to be excused for a minor mistake
   – Expressing outrage, as in "Well *excuse* me!"
   – Asking to get past someone

- Addressing a stranger's attention
- Asking someone to repeat themselves

FLY-TIPPING

Dumping rubbish at unauthorized places. This is often done by small commercial enterprises to avoid fees at the town dump.

GET/PUT THE WIND UP

An idiom that means to be frightened or very worried. For example: "Tell them your mother's a magistrate—that'll put the wind up them!"

GIRO

A system of transferring money from one bank account to another. This system was used to make payments to the unemployed. "Sorry, I can't pay you yet—I'm waiting for my giro to arrive." It's fading out in favor of EFT—electronic funds transfer. (Pronounced "JY-ro.")

GORDON BENNETT

An exclamation of incredulous surprise, anger, or frustration. Synonyms could include "damn," "damnations," or "hell." The original James Gordon Bennett was an early nineteenth-century American journalist noted for his "gutter journalism."

HANDBAGS AT TWENTY PACES

Slang for a half-hearted fight in which neither party wants to hurt the other.

HAPPY AS LARRY

To be extremely happy. It is believed that Larry was a boxer named Larry Foley, who sometime in the 1890s won a large cash prize for his final fight, but no one knows for certain.

HAVE A GO

Give it a try. Also, to become angry and shout at someone. See **Have a pop at.**

HAVE A POP AT

To insult, to rile.

HEATH ROBINSON

Something designed to perform a simple function, but which has an absurdly over-complicated design (like a Rube Goldberg drawing). Named after William Heath Robinson (1872–1944), a British cartoonist.

HER INDOORS

Slang for one's wife or female partner.

I'LL GIVE YOU WHAT FOR!

An old expression meaning, "I'll hurt you," born out of a response to disobedience. For example, an instructor gives an instruction. The respondent says, "What for?" The instructor replies "I'll give you what for!"

JOLLY GOOD

Very good.

JUST NOT CRICKET

When something that is unjust or just plain wrong is done to someone or something, it's "Just not cricket!" This comes from the game of cricket, which is regarded as a gentleman's game where fair play is of utmost importance.

KEEN AS MUSTARD

Enthusiastic.

KEEP A STIFF UPPER LIP

To keep up one's courage in the face of disappointment.

KEEP CALM AND CARRY ON

Not really a colloquialism, but the text of a very common poster during WWII, which is now widespread and readapted in vastly different contexts.

KEEP ONE'S END UP

To do your share of work or pay one's share.

KEEP ONE'S PECKER UP

To remain cheerful in a difficult situation.

KICK IN THE BOLLOCKS

A severe setback, a shock that forces you to stop for a while.

KNACKERED

Very tired, as in "Boy, am I knackered!" Since the late sixteenth century, "knackers" were those who slaughter horses. By the late eighteenth century, it was also used to describe a worn-out old horse.

KNOCKED FOR SIX

To be completely devastated by something. The term comes from the highest scoring action in cricket: where the ball is struck so hard that it reaches the boundary without touching the ground, scoring six runs (or points). For example, "He was knocked for six when his wife left him."

KNOCK UP

Pay attention, Americans! In the UK, this is to knock on someone's door. If you were staying at a hotel you might say to a friend "Just knock me up in the morning." But please note: It can also be used in the context more familiar to Americans, e.g., "She got knocked up by the lad who lives around the corner."

KNOW ONE'S ONIONS

Slang for knowledgeable and to be competent in your task. "He knows his onions!"

LOOK SMART

To be quick about something. "Look smart, it's almost time to go!" Also, to be stylish or fashionable.

LOSE YOUR BOTTLE

To lose your nerve, lose your determination, or have your courage disappear.

LOSE YOUR RAG

To lose your temper, to lose control of yourself. To be very, very angry.

LOVELY JUBBLY

Superb, great, excellent. Originally a marketing slogan for "Jubbly," a frozen orange drink, it was later popularized by the character Del Boy in the British comedy *Only Fools and Horses*.

MAD AS A HATTER

Completely crazy. This is often attributed to Lewis Carroll's *Alice Through the Looking Glass*, but the phrase predates the book. Dating from the early 1800s, the expression alludes to the tremors and nervous disorders caused by exposure to chemicals used in making felt hats.

MANKY

A term used in the North of England and in Scotland to describe anything broken, unpleasant, smelly, unwell, or under the weather. For example, "I'm limping 'cos I've got a manky foot." "Sorry about the smell, the bins are a bit manky."

MARDY

Another regional term, now predominately used in the North, meaning sulky, bad tempered, moaning. "Stop being so bloody mardy!" "It's just me, I'm feeling a bit mardy today."

MOGGY OR MOGGIE

A cat. Also, an affectionate nickname for a Morris Minor 1000, a distinctive, curvy, and compact car designed by Sir Alec Issigonis, who also designed the Mini. More than 1.6 million of these cars were sold between 1948 and 1971, and you can still see—and hear—them on Britain's streets.

MONKEY

Slang for five hundred pounds. It originates—like many expressions—from nineteenth-century India and the days of the British Empire. A five hundred rupee note featured a picture of a monkey, and the term was brought back to the UK and applied to local currency.

MUM'S THE WORD

Don't say anything about this, it's just between the two of us.

MUTTON DRESSED AS LAMB

A colloquialism referring to a middle-aged woman dressed too young for her age and looking conspicuous. (This was my mother's favorite English expression. She was disappointed that when she attempted to use it in America, people just looked at her puzzled.)

NEVER-NEVER

Slang for hire purchase, an installment plan. "He's buying it on the never-never" (implying that it will never actually be paid off). See **Hire purchase** page 192.

ONLY FOOLS AND HORSES

This is from a very popular TV sitcom about two brothers, Del Boy and Rodney Trotter, who live in a working-class area of London and are always trying to get money in silly, slightly illegal ways to avoid getting real jobs and paying taxes. Broadcast from 1981 to 2003, the series spawned a great number of phrases—including this one—that have worked their way into the popular vernacular.

OWN GOAL

To score an own goal is to make a self-inflicted mistake.

PENNY FOR THE GUY

This is the cry that children would make to ask for money to celebrate Guy Fawkes Night. Generally, kids would make an effigy of Guy Fawkes out of old clothes stuffed with straw or rags, and then parade it around the streets asking for "a penny for the guy." The money would be used to buy fireworks, and then when the bonfire was at its height of burning, the effigy would be hurled onto the fire. This practice has almost completely died out now, but the phrase lives on. See **Guy Fawkes Night** page 192.

PLAY SILLY BUGGERS

To act like a fool, to mess around. "Stop playing silly buggers, will ya!"

PUT THE FRIGHTENERS ON

To menace, threaten, or intimidate someone with the intention of frightening him or her into action or inaction.

RAG AND BONE MAN

In the early nineteenth century, one might have seen a man and pushcart moving through the streets of London or other major cities calling out for discarded clothing, bones, and other household items of low value that could then be resold to be remade into commercial products. Rags were made into poor-quality cloth called "shoddy," and any bones were rendered into glue. Like many early practices, this one has almost completely died out, but the term survives in the vernacular.

SAFE AS HOUSES

Something that is completely safe and secure with no risk of failure. The phrase alludes to the idea of a home being a safe haven or shelter.

SHE WHO MUST BE OBEYED
Reference to one's wife or girlfriend. Made popular by the 1970s TV series *Rumpole of the Bailey.*

SLAP-UP MEAL
A large, self-indulgent meal with food piled high on the plate. Usually used in conjunction with a special occasion or celebration.

SLING YOUR HOOK
Slang for "Go away."

SLOANE RANGER
A young, stereotypically blonde, woman who likes hanging out in Sloane Square, primarily on the Kings road in London. Being a Sloane Ranger indicates that you are of a generally reasonable class level; however, it also indicates a certain vacuous airhead-like attitude and snobbishness. The term was coined by British author Peter York in his 1975 book the *Official Sloane Ranger Handbook.*

SLOG ONE'S GUTS OUT
To work very hard.

SOME MOTHERS DO 'AVE 'EM
A reference to someone who is acting like an idiot, a buffoon. Also the title of a TV series based on a character with these characteristics.

SOMETHING FOR THE WEEKEND, SIR?

A discreet question asked by barbers enquiring whether a gentleman wished to purchase condoms. Although its origin is questionable, the expression was widely used in the UK in the second half of the twentieth century.

TAKING THE MICKEY

Lighthearted teasing, to make fun of a person or situation in a jocular (i.e., non-aggressive) manner. To mock. See **Banter** page 42.

TAKING THE PISS

A short form of "taking the piss out of someone," this has a wide range of meanings, from (relatively) lighthearted teasing among friends, to more aggressive mocking or ridicule. It can also be used to express a sense of disbelief at some perceived slight or insult. For example. "You're offering three hundred quid for my car? Are you taking the piss?"

TEN-A-PENNY

Describes something that is very common and therefore isn't worth very much. In America we might say, "A dime a dozen."

THROW ONE'S TOYS OUT OF THE PRAM

An expression of extreme anger bordering on infantile behavior.

TOOT-A-LOO (OR TOODALOO)

A short-term good-bye or "See you later."

TOSH

To speak a load of meaningless nonsense. "What a load of tosh!" To speak gibberish.

TURN SOMEONE OVER

To cheat, to rob someone, to attack or beat someone.

TWO SHAKES OF A LAMB'S TAIL

A colloquialism meaning very quickly, as in "He had it in his pocket in two shakes of a lamb's tail."

WELL AND TRULY

Something that is beyond repair or rectification, such as "Well and truly broken."

WIND IN HIS TAIL

Describing the state of being frightened or on high alert.

WIND UP

To play a joke on someone by telling them something that isn't true, or to tease beyond an acceptable level. "You need to stop winding me up, or I'm likely to explode."

– To deliberately and falsely create a situation that is very annoying. Often done in humor.

3.

Different Names and Pronunciations

ONE INTERESTING QUESTION, TO WHICH I DO NOT HAVE THE answer, is why so many objects in the UK have different names from their American counterparts. It is the result of cultural evolution, linguistic divergence, or just a desire to be different? To be sure, there have been technological developments in recent decades, which have brought the two languages closer, but even there some differences prevail. In the UK, people have "mobiles," while in the USA, people talk about their "cells." I have often said to people that "I haven't lost my American accent; I've lost my American vocabulary." I sometimes forget what things are called in the USA or even how to pronounce them. Take "cemetery," for example. In the USA, the word has four syllables, but in the UK, only three. To complicate matters—or perhaps to make everything more of an adventure as you travel around the UK—you will discover a fascinating plethora of local variations.

10 PIN BOWLING

In the USA, this is just bowling. The British include the "10 Pin" to differentiate it from other types of bowling, including lawn bowling and crown green bowling (the latter being played on a convex lawn.)

ABSEIL

To rappel. (Pronounced "AB-sale.")

ALUMINIUM

Same meaning as in the USA but spelled with an additional "i" and pronounced with five syllables, emphasis on the third. (Pronounced "Ah-lu-MIN-ee-um.")

AYE

It means "Yes." It is commonly used in Scotland.

BAIRN

A child. Used mainly in the North of England and in Scotland, the word comes from the old English "bearn."

BANTER

Playful teasing, usually between friends, but it can and does extend to good-natured, jocular exchanges between strangers. Sometimes abbreviated to "bants" or "bantz."

BARGEE

A member of a barge crew. *The Bargee* was a well-known 1964 film.

BAT

>Could be either a cricket bat or a ping pong paddle. Definitely not a baseball bat as Americans know it.

BESPOKE

>Something that is customized, not standardized. See **Made to measure** page 194.

BIG DIPPER

>Yes, it's the constellation in the sky, but this is also an older term for a roller coaster at an amusement park.

BILL, THE

>British slang for the police.

BIN LID

>The lid of a trash can. Many Liverpudlians use this unusual name for a bread roll. See **Bread roll** page 133.

BOLLOCKING

>To be punished severely or told off.

BONFIRE NIGHT

>See **Guy Fawkes** page 192.

BONE YARD

>Graveyard or cemetery.

BOXING DAY

The day after Christmas. December 26th is also St. Stephen's Day. St. Stephen has been associated throughout history with charitable acts. Traditionally, Boxing Day was a day off for the servants and laborers at the great country estate houses after the hustle and bustle of Christmas Day. The estate owners would box up gifts of food, money, and other valuables, and give them to their employees. The employees returned home with the gifts and spent the day with their own families.

BROADSHEETS

Full-size newspapers (as distinguished from half-size tabloids). Originally, broadsheets (e.g., the *Daily Telegraph*) and tabloid newspapers (e.g., the *Daily Star*) were differentiated by the quality of the reporting in addition to size and format. With the competition of the Internet news cycle, many of the most respected broadsheets have resorted to using techniques more similar to those used by the tabloid press. In fact, some former broadsheets are now printed in tabloid form (e.g., the *Daily Mail*).

BUGGY

A stroller.

BUTTY

A sandwich, as in "I'll have a bacon butty." Particularly used from Birmingham northward. See **Sarnie** page 156.

CASUALTY

Emergency room. *Casualty* is also a TV series about an emergency room. Also known as an "A&E" (Accident & Emergency). See **Surgery** page 215.

CATAPULT

A slingshot.

CEMETERY

A graveyard. (Pronounced "SEH-muh-tree" in Britain, with three syllables, not the four syllables used in the USA.)

COTTON BUD

A Q-tip. (Q-Tip is an American trademark.)

DRAUGHTS

Checkers. (Pronounced "drafts" or "drahfts.")

DUMMY

A pacifier.

EAR HOLE

An ear.

ESTATE AGENT

A real estate agent.

> The first house I bought in England was a mid-terrace, two up-two down, a little way outside of London. As the real estate agent was showing me around, he casually mentioned that it had been built in 1865.
>
> I said, "Oh, wow! So, this house was built the same year as the Civil War ended."
>
> "Nah, mate," he said, "that was in the 1600s."
>
> "No," I replied, "the *American* Civil War—it ended in 1865. Is there any kind of historical protection order on this house?"
>
> "No," he said. "It's not old enough."
>
> —M.H.

FATHER CHRISTMAS
Santa Claus.

FÊTE
Fair. A public event, often held outside, where you can take part in competitions and buy crafts and food. Often organized to collect money for a particular purpose. "The local church held a fête to raise money for the roof fund."

FLASK
Used here in much the same way as the USA (hip flask). In the UK, it can also mean a Thermos.

FLAT
An apartment.

FLICK KNIFE
A switchblade.

FOOTBALL

Soccer, not American football. The term soccer was created by students at the University of Oxford to distinguish between "rugger" football (Rugby) and "association" football (shortened to "soccer" and sometimes "socker"). American football, a sport that combines elements of both rugby and soccer, was originally called "gridiron football."

FORTNIGHT

Two weeks; fourteen days. "I'm going on holiday for a fortnight."

FRENCH LETTER

An old-fashioned term for a condom.

FRINGE

Bangs. Hair hanging straight down from the normal hair line over the forehead and usually trimmed to a straight edge.

FULL STOP

The punctuation mark known in the USA as a "period."

GRAFT

Hard work. "That's hard graft, that is!"

GUIDE DOG

Seeing eye dog. An animal specially trained to assist blind people.

HARE

An animal like a rabbit but larger with long ears, long legs, and a small tail. To go "haring off" somewhere is to go quickly.

HART

An archaic word for a stag deer. Usually only seen on pub signs these days, e.g., The White Hart.

HIRE

To rent something. A "tool hire shop" is somewhere you would go to rent a piece of equipment. A tuxedo hire shop, etc.

HOLIDAY

Time off from work including vacation time. Not defined as a specific day.

HOMELY

When used to describe a person, homely means quite pleasant-looking but perhaps a little plain. When used to describe a dwelling or other property, it means cozy, welcoming, and comfortable.

JCB

A generic term for the type of heavy equipment commonly used on building sites and civil engineering projects, e.g., diggers (backhoes), loaders, tractors, and excavators. The initials stand for founder Joseph Cyril Bamford, and the yellow logo is as familiar to Brits as the yellow/green logo of John Deere is to Americans.

JELLY

Jelly in the UK is what Americans call "Jell-O." Not to be confused with American jelly!

JUMBLE SALE

Rummage sale. Also known in the UK as a "bring and buy" sale, these events happen when people of the community bring secondhand possessions such as clothing or kitchen items to a central place, usually a church hall or community center, and sell them to others. These events are often held to benefit a charitable organization. See **Boot sales** page 96.

LADY BIRD

A ladybug.

LETTER BOX

A mailbox. See **Pillarbox** page 260.

LOO ROLL OR BOG ROLL

Toilet paper.

"English spelling would seem to have been designed chiefly as a disguise for pronunciation. It is a clever idea, calculated to check the presumption on the part of the foreigner."
—Jerome K. Jerome

MOBILE PHONE, MOBILE
> A cell phone.

NAPPIES
> Baby's diapers in both cloth and disposable form.

NOUGHT
> Zero, nothing, nil. (Rhymes with "ought.")

NOUGHTS AND CROSSES
> Tic-tac-toe.

NOWT
> Northern English dialect for nothing, e.g., "There's nowt
> on telly tonight." Conversely, 'owt' means "anything," hence
> "You don't get owt for nowt in this life," meaning "Nothing
> comes for free." (You may hear these words pronounced
> either "oat/note" or "out/nowt.")

NUT
> Your head. "He's doing my nut in!"

PAVEMENT
> Don't be fooled by this one! The pavement is the sidewalk.

PHONE BOX
> A telephone booth.

> "When the BBC first broadcast to the USA, it took a team of translators a week to figure out that 'Bangers and Mash' were not some veiled British threat."
>
> —Bill Clinton

PICKAXE

A pick for digging in the ground.

PITCH

A playing field.

PLUG HOLE

The drain in a sink or bathtub.

POST

Used generally in place of "mail" as in "Has the post arrived yet?"

QUEUE

A line of people or vehicles waiting for something. (Pronounced "cue.")

> "An Englishman, even if he is alone, forms an orderly queue of one."
>
> —George Mikes

RUBBER

An eraser. So, don't be shy about asking for one at the store!

SHATTERED

Very tired, too tired to continue.

SKIP

A dumpster.

SLEDGE

A sled for children to use in the snow.

SLEEPING POLICEMAN

A speed bump or humps. This is a cute euphemism for those wildly irritating road features that are supposed to slow down the traffic.

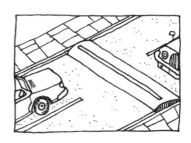

SOCCER

See **Football** page 47.

SPANNER

A wrench. Any wrench falls under this definition. Often heard in the phrase "to throw a spanner in the works."

STARTER

Appetizer, first course at dinner.

TIPP-EX

A proprietary brand name for typing correction fluid. Similar to the American brand "Wite-Out."

TITS

Tits are a species of small to medium sized birds that are visitors to gardens across England. There are six breeds: Blue, Coal, Willow, Marsh, Crested, and Great. They all have colorful plumage and are beloved by the English. (Full disclosure: The term in the UK also carries the common American meaning of a woman's breasts.)

TON (METRIC)

When Brits say "ton," they usually mean a metric ton. A metric ton is equal to 1,000 kilograms (abbreviated kg). Thus, a metric ton is slightly larger than a U.S. ton, which is 2,000 pounds. A metric ton is 2,204 pounds. To confuse matters further, there is also the imperial ton (or "long ton"), also known as a "British ton," which is slighter larger again, at 2,240 pounds. Got that?

TON (MONEY)

Slang for £100, one hundred pounds.

TONNE

An alternative spelling used to describe a metric ton. It is almost never used in American English, but it is widely used outside of the United States.

TORCH

> A flashlight.

TREAD, TROD

> To step on something. "He trod on my toes!" or "The path was well trodden."

TRUNCHEON

> A nightstick, or a blunt baton carried by policemen.

VAT

> Value-Added Tax. This is similar, but not identical, to sales tax in the USA. One big difference is that the tax is already included in the retail prices of products in stores—no additional charge is added at the checkout counter. When tourists leave the UK, they can often get a refund on any VAT they have paid.

WHINGE

> To complain a lot. To whine continuously.

ZED

> The last letter in the alphabet. One famous series of town-specific road atlases is entitled *A to Zed*.

4.

British Slang

THE DEFINITION OF SLANG VARIES FROM SOURCE TO SOURCE, but the generally accepted definition among non-linguists is language that is very informal—more so than colloquial language which is simply informal—or much below the standard level of education. Also, colloquialisms tend to be slightly longer and possibly forming a phrase, whereas slang is usually no more than two words. Hence, the dividing line between slang and colloquialisms is very narrow and perpetually moving. Many words start as slang and eventually become adopted as accepted language. Similarly, the precise meanings of slang terms vary across geography and through the ages. Because slang also encompasses vocabulary not in general use, many dialectal words are also thought of as slang.

Many slang terms emerged through a process called Hobson-Jobson, the assimilation of the sounds of a foreign word or words into an already existent language. For example, the Spanish *cucaracha* has become the English "*cockroach*," and the English "*riding coat*" has become the French *redingote*. This phenomenon is illustrated in British slang by English words such as "plonk," from the French *vin blanc*, and *hocus-pocus*, from the Latin *hoc est corpus*. Here are a few slang words commonly heard in the UK.

AGGRO

Aggravation, aggressive troublemaking.

BALLS-UP

A mistake leading to a negative outcome, a mess.

BARMY

Crazy or insane.

BARRY

Another term from the Scots, meaning "good" when exclaimed, or at least "okay."

BEASTLY

Nasty, unpleasant, particularly when describing somebody's behavior.

BELL

To call on the telephone, as in "Give me a bell."

BITS

Small things, or could refer to a person's genitals, as in "naughty bits!"

BLIMEY

An expression of surprise, annoyance, or strong feelings. Short for "gorblimey," a corruption of "God blind me."

BLINDER

An impressive or exciting action, thing, or person.

BLINDING

An expression of great approval. "It was a blinding performance" means "It was a great performance."

BLINKERED

Having a narrow-minded attitude or limited view about something.

BLOOMING (OR BLEEDING)

An adjective to add emphasis, like "bloody." "Blooming brilliant!"

BLOODY

A very old swear word that has become so familiar it is considered more fun than offensive. "Bloody" is British slang for "very." "Bloody brilliant!" It is also used to express anger or to emphasize what you are saying in a slightly rude way.

BOB

A shilling in old money (5p in today's currency) and no longer used. It has become a colloquialism as in "That'll cost you 10 bob" (50p).

BOBBYDAZZLER

Something or someone impressive.

BOLLITICS

Political correctness carried to absurdity.

BOGIE

A set of wheels and axles used to carry train cars. Two per car.
– Anything picked out of a person's nose. In the USA, the term is "booger." (Not to be confused with "bogey," the golf term.)

BONKERS

Just crazy. "That idea is bonkers!"

BOTHER

In the UK, this means to annoy someone or something by petty provocation. It can be used as a noun, as in "There was a spot of bother down the pub last night." Or as a verb: "There is a dog bothering the sheep!" It is also used to describe a religious adherent, as in "She's a bit of a God-botherer."

BOTTLE

To injure by thrusting a broken bottle into a person. "Bottle" is also British slang for courage or nerve.

BRASS

> In addition to the obvious, this word is sometimes sub-
> stituted for money. One popular colloquialism is "Where
> there's muck, there's brass," which means that dealing with
> anything disgusting or hazardous can be lucrative. A third
> meaning—one drawn from Cockney rhyming slang—is
> "prostitute." The term may come from "brass flute," "brass
> nail," or "brass tail," depending on who's telling the story.

BRICKING IT

> Being scared.

BRILL

> Short for "Brilliant!" it is slang for wonderful, exciting,
> fantastic.

CARVE UP

> To deliberately ruin someone's chances.
>   – To cut in front of another driver.

BUGGER

> This word has several meanings.
>   – A person or thing considered to be contemptible,
>   unpleasant, or difficult.
>   – A humorous or affectionate slang term for a man or
>   child.
>   – A person who engages in anal sex ("buggery").
>   – To ruin, complicate, or frustrate.

BUGGER ALL

Nothing. "That's left me with bugger all!" (Any time "bugger" is included in a phrase, it's a little ruder.)

BUGGER OFF

To go away (only, as mentioned above, slightly ruder).

BUNGALOW BILL

A slang term for a stupid man that derives from the Beatles song, "The Continuing Story of Bungalow Bill."

BUNK OFF

To play truant, to be absent.

CAT'S WHISKERS

An expression meaning that someone or something is the very best, excellent, and appealing. Can also be used sarcastically as in "She thinks she's just the cat's whiskers," when she is really just the opposite.

CAUGHT SHORT

To be caught with a sudden urge to go to the toilet and nowhere to relieve yourself.

CHAP

A man, particularly of gentlemanly nature.

CHEAP AS CHIPS

Very affordable.

CHEEKY
Something or someone who is charmingly rude or disre-spectful in an amusing way. Often used affectionately in the expression "He's a cheeky monkey."

CHEERIO
Used generally as a friendly way to say good-bye. Also sometimes used as a greeting.

CHEESED OFF
Bored, disgusted, or angry.

CHOKEY
Prison.

CHUFFED
Very delighted, pleased.

CHUNNEL
The Channel Tunnel.

CLANGER
A glaring mistake.

CLAPPED OUT
Broken down; at the end of an item's use. Usually used to describe machinery.

CLAPPERS

"Going like the clappers" means going very fast. Usually applied to driving but could be used for anything moving rapidly.

CLEVER-CLOGS

A know-it-all.

COCK-UP

A mistake.

CODSWALLOP

A description of something that someone has just said as nonsense or untrue, "What a load of codswallop!"

CRACKING

Extremely good. "We had a cracking day!"

CRAIC

A Gaelic term that has now entered common parlance meaning "fun," "entertainment," and "enjoyable interaction with others." "Tonight was a great craic." (Pronounced "crack.")

CREAM CRACKERED

To be very tired out. Comes from the rhyming slang for "knackered."

CRIKEY

An exclamation of surprise.

DAFT

Frivolous, giddy, insane. "That's just daft!" More affectionate today than it was in the past.

DEAR

In addition to a term of endearment, in the UK this can also mean expensive. "I do like venison from time to time, but it can be a little dear."

DICKY

Faulty, often used to describe ailments, as in "I've got a dicky ticker" (a bad heart).

DICKY BIRD

Complete silence: Not a sound, not an utterance. The term dates from at least the eighteenth century, when it appeared in the *London Evening News*, May 1766.

DO ONE'S HEAD IN

To drive insane, annoy. "She's doin' my head in!"

DO ONE'S NUT

To lose one's temper, become very angry.

DODGY

A word with various meanings. It's probably used most often to describe something vaguely (or definitely) dishonest: "He's involved in dodgy deals." "He's a bit of a dodgy geezer." It can also mean unsafe or dangerous: "We didn't know the neighborhood but could tell it was a dodgy location." And thirdly, it can be used to describe something of less-than-perfect quality: "Be careful driving that car, the brakes are a bit dodgy."

DOOBRY

Something unspecified whose name is either forgotten or not known.

DOSH

Money.

DUCKY

A term of endearment, particularly for family, women and children.

EARACHE

Incessant chatter, complaining, or nagging.

EARWIG

To eavesdrop. "He's earwigging on the conversation at the next table."

EASY-PEASY

British slang for very easy.

EFF AND BLIND, (EFFIN AND BLINDIN)

To use obscene language.

FAFF

To "faff about" means to behave in a confused or disorganized manner.

FANCY

A soft desire for something, including people, food and/or objects, activities, things. "I fancy a cup of tea now."

FANNY ABOUT

Mess around or waste time.

FAG

A very old word in English that has several meanings:
- Cigarette. "I'm stepping out for a fag."
- An offensive word for a gay man. The term didn't really come in to use in that context until the early 1920s, giving rise to much confusion amongst English tourists abroad asking, "Have you got a fag, mate?"

- Hard drudgery work that makes you tired, as in "It was such a fag."
- An English public schoolboy who serves as a servant to an older schoolmate. To serve as a fag.

FAG-END
A cigarette butt.

FIN
A five-pound note.

FIVER
£5, five pounds. Also referred to as a "deep-sea diver" in cockney rhyming slang.

FLIPPIN
A negative adjective, a softer version of a well-known expletive, "Flippin heck!"

FOOTY
Football.

FRONT
Cheek, effrontery. "He's got a lot of front, he does!"

FULL MONTY
The complete amount.

GAFF

A mistake, an error. Also, an Irish slang word for "house," it's commonly used today by Londoners and residents of southern England, as in "Meet me round my gaff in half an hour."

GEE-GEE

A horse.

GIVE A BELL

See **Bell** page 56.

GOBSHITE

To speak complete nonsense. Northern British slang for a contemptible person.

GOBSMACKED

To be so surprised or astounded that your mouth hangs open.

GROTTY

Unpleasant, nasty, unattractive, poor quality, in bad condition, unsatisfactory, or useless.

GUBBINS

Paraphernalia of something.

GUTTED

Devastated, deeply disappointed, saddened, shocked.

HAD OVER

To be tricked, duped, or deceived.

HEN NIGHT (PARTY)

A female social gathering, especially a pre-wedding celebration. The female version of a bachelor party.

JAMMY

A situation that is pleasant; desirable. "Jammy" is also British slang for lucky.

JUMBLY

See **Jumble sale** page 49.

KIP

Sleep. "I'm off for a kip now." Also, a place to sleep.

KNACKERS

Slang for testicles.

LOADS-A-MONEY

Someone flaunting excessive wealth.

LOLLY

Ill-gotten money. Usually applied to the results of a robbery.

LURGI

An unspecified, unknown illness. "He's got the lurgi!"

MALARKEY

Nonsense. "What's all that malarkey they were discussing?"

MEAN

To be stingy to the point of miserly.

MINTED

Very wealthy.

MUCK

Manure, often used in the phrase "Common as muck."

NAFF

Something that is rubbish, useless; inferior; in poor taste.

NAFF OFF

A demand to "go away."

NAFFED-OFF

An expression of being fed up. "I'm naffed-off with all these office politics."

NAFFING

A negative adjective meaning "very."

NANA

A child's or young person's word for their grandmother.

NARKY

Annoyed, ill tempered. "Don't get narky with me!"

NAVVY

A manual laborer; an unskilled construction worker or road digger. Historically applied to the Irish workers who dug the canals in the UK.

NEWS OF THE WORLD

Gossip, word of mouth. A lingering reference to *News of the World*, a tabloid published in the UK from 1843 to 2011.

NICK

There are several meanings applied to this word, most to do with the police.

  - to arrest: "Right, you've been nicked."
  - to steal something: "Be careful, someone might nick your purse."
  - a prison or a police station: "They've got him down the nick."

NIFFY

Having an unpleasant smell. As in "Something smells a bit niffy in here!"

NIP INTO

To stop somewhere for a short period of time. "I just have to nip into the post office."

NOT ON

Something that is unacceptable. "His behavior is just not on!"

ODDS AND SODS

Slang for bits and pieces.

OFF YOU GO

To get started or get on your way, as in "It's time for school—off you go."

ON ABOUT

As part of "What are you on about?" with "on" replacing the word "talking."

ON YOUR BIKE

A demand to go away.

OOJAMAFLIP

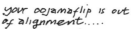

your oojamaflip is out of alignment.....

A nonsensical word, "oojamaflip" is slang for an unspecified or un-nameable thing, something you can't remember the name of. (Pronounced "OO-ja-ma-flip.)

PICCADILLY CIRCUS

A very busy, crowded situation. "It's like Piccadilly Circus in there."

PIECE OF PISS (PIECE OF PUDDING)
Something very easy to accomplish.

PISS OFF
Go away, as an instruction or an action. "The cops are coming—we'd better piss off."

PISSED
Drunk.

PISSED OFF
Upset, angry.

PLODDING
Methodical, uninspiring progress.

PONCE ABOUT (AROUND)
To behave in a showy and irresponsible manner.

POPPYCOCK
Nonsense, rubbish talk.

POSH
Reference to someone or something elegant or high class. According to legend, this derives from tickets for first-class cabins on old steam liners to India, which supposedly said, "Port Out Starboard Home," thus creating the acronym POSH. This theory has been widely debunked.

POXY

Adjective applied to anything considered to be rubbish, crass, inferior, worthless.

PUKKA

Old British slang for authentic, first-rate, genuine; made popular again in recent years by the TV chef Jamie Oliver. "That's a pukka pie!"

PULL YOUR SOCKS UP

An admonishment to start working or improve your work or behavior, because it is not good enough. "She needs to pull her socks up if she is to make a success of her career."

QUID

One pound sterling (money).

QUIDS IN

In the money, in profit.

RANK

Disgusting, revolting.

RAZZLE

"On the razzle" means a spree or good time. Usually associated with alcohol.

RAZZLE-DAZZLE
Slang for a noisy or showy fuss or activity.

READIES
Available cash. "I'm a bit low on the readies tonight."

RECKON
To think about something. "I reckon it's a good investment."

RIPPING
Excellent; splendid.

ROLLER
A Rolls-Royce car.

ROUND THE HOUSES
A long and futile mission. "I've been round the houses looking for that!"

SCHTUM
To keep silent about something, as in "Keep schtum about this!" Used in the East End vernacular, its origin is German Yiddish.

SCORE
Twenty of something, usually money, as in "That will cost you a score, mate!"

SENT DOWN

To be sentenced to imprisonment.

SHAGGED

To be worn out, tired, exhausted. See **Shag** page 295.

SHUFTY

To have a look (from the Arabic for "look").

SIR ALEC

A pint of Guinness.

SKINT

Lacking money, poor, as
in "I'm completely skint at
the moment!"

Down to my last penny. I'm skint!

SKIVE

To avoid working, either by doing as little as possible
("Where's Steve?" "Probably skiving over at the warehouse.")
or by staying away completely ("He's not sick! He's skiving
off today.").

SLAG OFF

To denigrate, criticize, or insult. To verbally put down
someone or something.

SLAMMED

Drunk, intoxicated.

75

SLAPPER

A derogatory term referring to a woman who is a bit sexually promiscuous.

SMASHING

A positive exclamation meaning "really good."

SNAP

A phrase meaning "Same thing happened to me!"

SNIP

A bargain or a great value purchase. "It's a snip at that price." It is also a slang term for a vasectomy. "With four kids now, I'm getting the snip."

SOD-ALL

Nothing. "There's sod-all left for us!"

SOD OFF

Go away. "Just sod off, will ya?"

SPAG BOL

Spaghetti Bolognese.

SQUIFFY

To be lightly intoxicated, delightfully tipsy.

STARKERS

Completely naked. "There he stood, completely starkers!"

STREWTH

An exclamation of surprise or frustration.

SUSS (SUSS OUT)

To work something out, to investigate, to understand, to discover, to deduce. "Suss" is slang for knowledge, understanding.

TA!

An informal "Thank you!"

TIP

The garbage dump.

TOMMYROT

Nonsense. "He was talkin' complete tommyrot!"

TOP WHACK

The most, the highest possible amount. "He paid top whack for that car."

TURN OVER

To rob. To raid or search a premise. (Not an apple pie from McDonald's!)

TWIG

To understand.

TENNER

A ten-pound note.

UNI

Short word for university.

WICKED

Cool or exciting.

YONKS

An age, a long time.

5.

Pejoratives, Insults, and Derision

THE BRITISH ARE WELL KNOWN FOR SAYING ONE THING AND meaning another, as if their true intentions are hidden behind a veil of social politeness. True participants of English culture, who know how to read the code, will know what they mean anyway. To straight-speaking Americans, this simultaneously smacks of duplicitous deceit and also sets them up as easy targets. Many Americans, fascinatingly, feel that insults are more effective when done in an English accent. This hints at an underlying mistrust of anything that anyone with an English accent says. It is not a coincidence that many of the best cinema villains are British. Anthony Hopkins, James Mason, Donald Pleasance, Peter Cushing, Christopher Lee, and Alan Rickman immediately spring to mind.

I was flabbergasted the first time I watched *Prime Minister's Question Time* on television. The exchange of insults and sharp innuendo delivered in a framework of elaborate courtesy must be a theatrical farce, I thought. Here's just one example: "Will the right honorable member explain to the English people how this legislation won't destroy our way of life in this country?" One American observer described proceedings as "A gift-wrapped dose of poison" as he left the Visitors' Gallery of the Houses of Parliament.

British insults are acerbic combinations of wit, sarcasm, double entendre, and two-sided compliments. These make the art of British insult particularly cutting while simultaneously interesting and unusually funny. Winston Churchill was famous for his quick and biting wit, and several of his more famous retorts are included here.

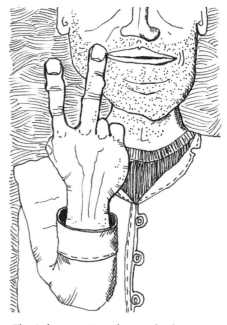

The infamous 'Two fingered salute' or a V-sign, page 313

Note: Some entries in here are neither PG nor even PC, so be forewarned!

AIRY-FAIRY

Used to describe someone who is (or whose ideas are) not strong, unrealistic, vague, weak.

ANKLE-BITERS

Children. Usually used by people who do not have children.

ARSE-LICKER

A sycophant, one who acts obsequiously toward someone important to gain an advantage.

AWAY WITH THE FAIRIES

Referring to someone who is out of touch with reality or gives the impression of being crazy or in dreamworld.

BERK

An annoying idiot. Can be applied to yourself as well. "I felt a right berk when I lost my ticket."

BIG GIRL'S BLOUSE

A weak, ineffectual, cowardly, or oversensitive man.

BINT

A derogatory word for a woman.

BLIGHTER

Someone whose behavior ruins things or situations.

BOILER

An unkind term for an unattractive woman.

"The only consolation I can find in your immediate presence is your ultimate absence."

—Shelagh Delaney

CHANCER

An unscrupulous or dishonest opportunist who is prepared to try any dubious scheme for making money or furthering his own ends.

CHAV

A derogatory term used to describe a young hooligan who wears designer sportswear, drinks too much, and starts fights. A chav (rhymes with "have") is usually seen as poorly educated and lower class. The etymology of the term is generally accepted to be from the Romany word *chavi* meaning "child." The claim that it actually stands for "Council House and Violent" is a great example of a "backronym," a made-up explanation of a word's origin. Regional terms with a similar meaning include "Ned" (Scotland) and "Scally" (northwest England). See **Yob** page 92 and **Hooligan** page 84.

CHEESE-EATING SURRENDER MONKEYS

Sometimes shortened to just "surrender monkeys," this pejorative term is used to describe the French people. The UK has never forgiven them for their surrender to the Germans in 1941. When, in 1995, an episode of *The Simpsons* used the phrase, many members of the British populace seized upon it as yet another way to insult an entire nation.

DAFT COW

A dumb, large woman.

DEAD FROM THE NECK UP

Referring to a particularly stupid person.

ESSEX GIRL

A derogatory characterization of a young woman from the county of Essex, in southeast England, who is materialistic, attention seeking, and obsessed with sex. It's not a realistic description and is thus unfortunate.

> "Mr. Churchill, I care neither for your politics nor your mustache."
> "Do not distress yourself, madam. You are unlikely to come into contact with either."
> —Unidentified woman and Winston Churchill

FROG

Yet another derogatory term for a Frenchman. Britain and France have had a love-hate relationship for centuries, frequently invading one another (the French port of Calais was an English city from 1360 to 1588), stealing vocabulary, and trading insults. As with many other national nicknames, this mildly derogatory term derives from a favored food, the French being known for eating frogs' legs. The French, in turn, refer to Brits as *rosbifs*, after roast beef.

FUZZY-WUZZY

A derogatory term for a black native of various countries, particularly someone with tightly curled hair. "Fuzzy-Wuzzy" is also slang for a Sudanese soldier. This term was used by nineteenth-century British colonial soldiers for the members of the Hadendoa, an East African nomadic tribe.

GANNET

A gluttonous or greedy person. Usually applied to eating with speed like the gannet bird.

GORMLESS

Describes someone with a complete lack of common sense.

GREEN WELLY BRIGADE

A derogatory phrase for wealthy upper-middle-class townspeople who visit the country on weekends.

GYPSIES OR GYPSY

A pejorative term for a nomadic race of people who travel from place to place, usually in caravans, rather than living in one place. In the UK, not all nomadic people are Romany; some are ethnic Irish and Scottish itinerant workers. See **New Age Traveller** page 212, **Pikey** page 88, **Traveller** page 217.

HARD ARSE

An unyielding, severe, tough, uncompromising person.

HOOLIGAN

A noisy, violent person who fights or causes damage in public places. In the UK, hooliganism is almost exclusively confined to football. See **Yob** page 92.

HOORAY HENRY

An offensive and rowdy upper-middle-class young man.

> "If I were your wife, I'd put poison in your coffee."
> "If I were your husband, I'd drink it."
> —Nancy Astor and Winston Churchill

JACK THE LAD

A self-assured, cocky young man.

JOBSWORTH

An official who upholds petty rules at the expense of common sense. A person who is very pedantic at work.

KILTIE

A person who wears a kilt, and also a slightly pejorative term for a Scotsman.

KNOCKING ON

Slang for getting old. "She's knocking on a bit!" Supposedly derived from the phrase "knocking on heaven's door."

LADDETTE

A swaggering, drunken, uncouth young woman.

LARD-ARSE

A derogatory term for a fat person.

LIGGER

A freeloader, a hanger-on. One who takes advantage of free travel and parties offered by companies for publicity purposes.

LIKE A DOG WITH TWO DICKS

Sexually promiscuous, with the implication that the person cannot control his or her sexual appetite; having animal-like urges.

LIMP-WRISTED

Feeble or effeminate.

LITTER LOUT

A person who drops refuse in public places.

LORD MUCK

Slang for a man perceived to be behaving high-handedly, a snob.

LUVVIE

A pejorative term for an actor or actress.

LYCRA LOUT

A derogatory term for an arrogant, road-hogging cyclist. See **Cycle lane** page 99.

MAD AS A BAG OF FERRETS

Crazy.

MINGER

> An ugly or filthy-minded person, usually with an implication of poor hygiene or body odor.

MUPPET

> A dimwitted or inept person.

MUNTER

> An ugly person, usually applied to women. Also spelled "munta."

NAMBY (NAMPY-PAMBY)

> A weak, cowardly person. Eccentric, a little crazy, or odd.

> "No one can be as calculatedly rude as the British, which amazes Americans, who do not understand studied insult and can only offer abuse as a substitute."
>
> —Paul Gallico

NUMPTY

> An idiot.

NUTTER

> Someone who is crazy. Can also be used to describe a person who is wild and unpredictable, as in "He's a real nutter!"

OIK

A derogatory term for a person regarded as inferior because of being ignorant, ill-educated, or lower class. (Pronounced "o-yik.")

OLD BAT

A grumpy old person, usually female. A term of derision to indicate that the person is annoying or unpleasant.

OLD GIT

A cantankerous old person.

PADDY

A pejorative term for someone from Ireland.

PEDO

A pedophile.

PIKEY

A gypsy. Also slang for a vagrant. See **Gypsies** page 84, **New Age Travelers** page 212, **Travelers** page 217.

PILLOCK

Someone who is an idiot or a fool. Someone who is unbearably stupid.

PLONKER

A fool or a stupid person. Made popular by Del Boy in the TV series *Only Fools and Horses.*

PLUG-UGLY (PUG-UGLY)

> Very, very ugly or hideous.

POMMY

> A pejorative term for a person from Britain, used by Australians and New Zealanders. There are a couple of theories as to the source of this term. One is that "pomegranate" sort of rhymes with "immigrant." Another possible etymology is that it's sort of an acronym for "Prisoner of Mother England."

PONCE

> An ostentatious, effeminate male.

> "Two tickets reserved for you for the first night of my new play. Bring a friend. If you have one."
> "Cannot make the first night. Will come to the second night. If you have one."
> —George Bernard Shaw and Winston Churchill

PRAT

> A frequently used insult meaning a stupid or badly behaved person.

QUEER

> Historically slang for a homosexual, in the UK this also means to feel slightly ill: "I was feeling rather queer after departing from the hovercraft."

RODNEY

An upper-class male idiot.

ROTTER

A worthless, unpleasant, or despicable person.

SASSENACH

A pejorative used by Irish and Scots referring to a person coming from England. An anglicized form of the Scottish Gaelic word "sasunnach," meaning "Saxon." (Pronounced "SASS-eh-nack.")

SCROTE

An unpleasant person. (If you think you know the origin of this word, you are probably right.)

SCRUBBER

A coarse and sexually acquiescent or promiscuous woman.

SHEEPSHAGGER

An offensive term for a countryman, often a Welshman.

SHIRTLIFTER

A derogatory term for a male homosexual.

SLAPHEAD

A balding person.

> "Winston, you're drunk."
> "Bessie, you're ugly. But tomorrow I shall be sober."
> —Bessie Braddock and Winston Churchill

SMARMY

Obsequious, condescending, or flattering with ulterior motives.

SMEG

A foolish or dirty person. An idiot.

SPIV

A man or boy who makes a living by underhanded dealings or swindling; could be a black marketeer.

TIGHT-ARSE

Slang for a mean, selfishly frugal, stingy, person.

TOFFEE-NOSED

Snobby. Used as an adjective. "Toffee-nosed git!"

TOFF

A rich, well-dressed, or upper-class person, usually a man.

TOSSER

Someone who masturbates a lot. See **Wanker** page 298.

TROLLOP

A disreputable lady of questionable morals.

TWAT

A foolish or despicable person. A harsh insult but not quite swearing; more extreme than "prat."

TWIT

Slang for an idiotic, foolish, or absurd person.

WALLY

An idiot or imbecile.

WAZZOCK (WASSOCK)

Someone so dumb they can only do manual labor. Used in Yorkshire.

WET

Used to describe someone of weak character or who is unable to state a strong opinion.

WOOFTER

A male homosexual.

WURZEL

Someone from Bristol.

YOB (YOBBO)

A man, usually young, rough, loud, and behaving badly.

6.

Driving and Transportation

FEW FEATURES OF A VISIT TO THE UK FRIGHTEN AMERICANS more than "driving on the wrong side of the road." In the UK, the driver sits on the right-hand side of the car, the passenger on the left. This often means that American passengers must fight an overwhelming urge to hit a non-existent brake pedal. The transfer of skills from left to right is usually fairly smooth, but things can get more challenging at roundabouts and junctions. Fortunately, reasonably good signage assists the newly arrived driver with reminders like "KEEP LEFT EXCEPT TO PASS." Another good thing is that the brake and accelerator pedals are in the same configuration as in left-hand-drive cars. At least you don't have to worry about stepping on the gas when you mean to brake! The number of motorists unaccustomed to right-hand driving has increased because of the UK's acceptance of all European Union driver's licenses. Since EU drivers all drive on the right in their home countries, they're making all the same mistakes that Americans do.

The British have some driving customs that American visitors may find insane. Parking in the wrong direction on the wrong side of the road is common. Parking on sidewalks is becoming less common, but you might still see pedestrians squeezing around cars blocking their paths. On the other hand, the countryside has enchanting winding lanes that, except for the addition of blacktop, have changed little in hundreds of years.

Walking has its challenges, too. London has so many international tourists that at pedestrian crossing points there are signs painted on the road surface saying, "LOOK LEFT" or "LOOK RIGHT" to help prevent people from stepping into oncoming traffic because they might otherwise look the wrong way.

My advice is: Just keep saying, "Sitting on the right—driving on the left." If that's not enough help, take the train or call a rideshare.

"A" ROAD

A wide, paved road with drains, not a freeway. Roads whose numbers are prefixed with the letter "A." These roads are the busiest and most direct main roads apart from motorways. "A" Road numbers can be one, two, three, or four digits long.

AA

The Automobile Association. One of a number of auto assistance clubs or services. Other major ones include the RAC and Green Flag.

ARTICULATED LORRY

A semi-truck with a separate cab and trailer; commonly referred to as an "artic."

"B" ROAD

Secondary roads whose number is prefixed with the letter "B" and which have no curbs or drains. They are third in the British road-numbering scheme, following "M" (freeways) and "A" (primary roads). "B" Road numbers are never more than four digits long.

BACK DOUBLES

Residential streets running off main roads. May also refer to a shortcut. Also known as a "rat run."

BEDFORD VAN

A brand of ubiquitous vans in the UK from the 1960s through the early 1990s. Manufactured by Vauxhall Motors, the Bedford Van was second only to the Ford Transit in popularity. Vauxhall produced a range of full-size panel vans without side windows, used mainly by workmen, until production ceased in 1991. See **White van men** page 113.

BELISHA BEACON

A flashing yellow globe indicating a pedestrian crossing. Possibly the most British of all roadside features. They were named for Leslie Hore-Belisha, the Minister of Transport from 1934 to 1937, who oversaw their introduction. While they are becoming scarce these days, having been replaced by pedestrian-controlled traffic signals, they do still exist—their globe-shaped lights enhanced with a ring of LED lights.

BLACK MARIA

A prison van or police vehicle used to transport prisoners. Commonly called a "paddy wagon" in the USA. (Pronounced "black ma-RYE-uh.")

BLACK SPOT

A colloquial term used to describe a particularly dangerous junction or section of road where accidents frequently occur. Often also referred to as an "accident black spot."

BONNET

A car hood, in addition to a woman's brimmed hat.

BOOT

A trunk of an automobile. Also, of course, footwear.

BOOT SALES

Meetings of cars where individuals sell all manner of goods—some of it legal—from their car boots.

BOX JUNCTION

A traffic intersection marked with crossing lines into which a vehicle must not enter unless it can exit the other side. In the USA, this is referred to as "the box."

BOY RACER

A reckless, young male car driver who drives fast and dangerously trying to impress.

BREAKERS YARD

An automobile junkyard.

BUS PASS (SENIOR)

Although there is a generic meaning to the term "bus pass," in the UK it generally refers to a card given to senior citizens that allows for free travel on local buses. In Scotland, this benefit is given through the National Entitlement Card (NEC) and in Wales it is via the Concessionary Travel Card (CTC).

BYPASS

A diversion of a major road to carry traffic around a built-up area, in order to improve the journey of through traffic as well as improve the environment along the original route.

CAMPER VAN

A self-contained, drivable camper equipped with beds and cooking equipment so that you can live, cook, and sleep in it. It is smaller than an American motorhome and may or may not contain a bathroom. See **Caravan** page 98.

CAR PARK

A parking lot.

CARAVAN

An unpowered trailer pulled by another vehicle. It may be used for camping purposes but not necessarily. Some of these can be quite large. See **Camper van** page 97.

CARRIAGE

A train car.

CARRIAGEWAY

The lane of a road, as in "dual carriageway" or "narrow carriageway."

CENTRAL RESERVATION

The median strip of a motorway or multilane highway.

CHARABANG (CHARABANC)

The horse-drawn charabang was a common vehicle in England during the early part of the twentieth century. It was used for large parties and was popular for sightseeing tours to the country or the seaside. The charabang originated in France in the early nineteenth century. The term was carried over to motorized coaches in the twentieth century but has largely fallen out of use today. (pronounced "SHARE-a-bang.")

CIRCULAR ROAD

Also known as a "ring road," this thoroughfare goes around a city or town either fully or partially. There can be inner circular roads, and in large cities like London, there may be several. See **Ring road** page 109.

CITY CENTRE

The busiest part of a city, where most of the shops, government services, and businesses are located. You will see this term on street signs. In the USA, this would be called "downtown."

CLOSE

A cul-de-sac or alley. Not a through road.

CONGESTION CHARGING

Introduced in February of 2003 in London, fees on vehicles that travel through central London between the hours of 8:00 a.m. and 7:00 p.m.

CYCLE LANE

A dedicated lane for cyclists along urban roads, known in the USA as a "bike lane." These are often poorly designed, with sudden disappearances and reappearances. Frequent noncompliance with the traffic laws governing them, by both motorists and cyclists, is another problem. In the

UK, cyclists are not allowed on sidewalks and must share the road with motorists and trucks. This creates ongoing tension among users and frequent altercations. I gave up cycling when I moved to the UK because of its crazy level of danger.

DIVERSION

A detour or an alternate way of driving somewhere when a road is closed.

DOUBLE YELLOW

A set of two yellow lines running along the side of a roadway to indicate that there is no parking in that section of the road. Often ignored by delivery drivers.

DUAL CARRIAGEWAY

Any road in the UK with an area of land in the middle that divides lanes of traffic moving in opposite directions. In the USA, these are called "divided highways."

DYNAMO

A device that changes the energy of movement into electricity. A dynamo on a bicycle generates enough electricity to power its lights.

ESCAPE ROAD (ESCAPE LANE)

A short road, usually lined with a deep layer of gravel, found at the bottom of a steep hill to catch runaway vehicles that are unable to stop. Often called a "runaway truck ramp" in the USA.

ESTATE CAR

A station wagon. In the United States, these would be considered "cross-over SUVs." Many have trunks, which is quite different from traditional station wagons.

E-TYPE

The Jaguar E-Type, known in the USA as the Jaguar XK-E.

FLYOVER

An overpass that carries one road over another.

GIVE WAY

In traffic terminology, this is to yield right of way.

GRANNY LANE

Slang for the left lane (slow lane) of a motorway. In the USA, it is the far-outside lane on the right.

GYRATORY SYSTEM

A large and complex roundabout accommodating several roads and containing several lanes. The most famous gyratory system is the Hangar Lane Gyratory in west London, often known by its nickname, "Malfunction Junction." It's terrifying traffic madness until you memorize it.

HACKNEY CARRIAGE

A taxi. The first licensed taxis were in the Hackney area of London, and the name carried over to apply to all licensed vehicles. More commonly referred to as "black cabs" or "black taxis," although these days they can be any color. The original Hackney carriage was a horse-drawn carriage, and the name has stuck. Black taxis can be hailed down on the street, or they can be pre-booked. Minicabs have been licensed since 2001. The main difference between the two is that black cabs can be flagged down, whereas minicabs must, by law, be pre-booked (although that may not stop the more unscrupulous operators looking for business).

HARD SHOULDER

An auxiliary lane on the left of the highway, set aside for stopped vehicles and emergency services to ensure that the main running lanes on the highway remain free from obstructions. On motorways, it is illegal to stop on a hard shoulder except in an emergency.

HERITAGE RAILWAYS

Railways that have been saved by enthusiasts and volunteers from destruction and abandonment. When railways began to be deemed old-fashioned, the British government attempted to eliminate smaller lines in favor of motorways. The donations and efforts of thousands of people who didn't want to see them disappear have kept more than four hundred of these heritage lines open to the public.

HIGHWAY CODE

First introduced in 1931, the Highway Code is a set of rules governing the use of roadways in England, Scotland, Wales, and Northern Ireland. It dictates speed limits, definition of road types, all driving actions, types of vehicles permitted on the roads, and safety standards. Everything there is to know about road rules and regulations is in the Highway Code, which is printed as a study book and also available online. All student drivers must memorize the Highway Code in order to pass their driver's test and receive a license.

INDICATOR

A car's turn signal.

JAG

A Jaguar automobile.

JUGGERNAUT

A very large container truck. A word of Indian origin that may also refer to any massive vehicle (such as a steam locomotive) or to any other enormous entity with powerful crushing capabilities. In the UK, it's only used to describe large, heavy trucks. Even the largest of the heavy trucks in the UK are not as large as most of the big rigs in the USA.

L-PLATE

A sign, self-adhesive or magnetic, with a red letter L, attached to the front and rear of a car, to warn other vehicles that the driver of that car is a "learner" or student driver.

LAY-BY

An area off an "A" Road or a "B" Road into which a truck or car may pull and rest for a while. There are no structures or toilet facilities, but some lay-bys have unofficial mobile trailers or vans selling coffee or sandwiches. A lay-by is usually not as developed as a rest stop in the USA. Motorways, however, have "services": gas stations and restaurants.

LEVEL CROSSING

A railroad crossing on a road.

LITRE

A metric unit of volume that is one thousand cubic centimeters. It is equal to 1.76 British pints or 2.11 American pints. All gasoline in the UK is dispensed in litre units, but fuel efficiency is still generally discussed in terms of miles per gallon. Milk is sold in litres, but, echoing the old one-, two-, and four-pint measures, you'll see cartons in supermarkets marked 568ml, 1.136l, 2.272l, etc. Draft beer, reassuringly, has yet to succumb to metrication, so you can still enjoy a pint.

LOLLIPOP MAN OR LADY

A school crossing guard. The nickname comes from the large lollipop-shaped sign that they use to stop traffic. Take them quite seriously … the law certainly does.

LORRY

A truck. The term usually refers to a fairly large vehicle.

LOW EMISSION ZONE (LEZ)

A scheme introduced across Greater London in 2008 that imposes fines on the most polluting large vehicles. It is part of an experimental scheme that includes similar zones across Europe. See **ULEZ** page 112.

"M" ROAD

A freeway, or motorway.

MACADAM

Small chips of stone bound together by asphalt or tar and compressed into a road surface. Named after John McAdam (1756–1836), the Scottish engineer who invented it. Also known as "tarmac." (Pronounced "ma-CAD-um.")

MAGIC ROUNDABOUT

A fabled, almost mythical entity discussed in hushed tones by American drivers in the UK. It is a quite large roundabout surrounded by several smaller ones to accommodate multiple roads or streets accessing it. The resulting street signs clearly look like a carousel (roundabout)

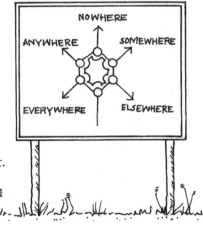

or a clock face. Nearly every city of any size lays claim to the original magic roundabout, including Hemel Hempstead,

High Wycombe, Swindon, Bristol, and Colchester. It is also the name of a 1970s television series for children with a well-known character named Zebedee.

MINI

An icon of British culture, the Mini is a very small, inexpensive car first produced in 1959. The Mini Cooper was created as a performance rally car. The movie *The Italian Job* featured several Minis in its storyline, and Austin Powers drove a Mini. The award-winning Mini is now produced by BMW and is considerably larger—and more comfortable—than the original.

MINICAB

See **Hackney carriage** page 102.

> "As long as you know that 'to let' means to rent and not a place to pee, you're all set to travel in the UK. The lifts and the boots and everything else don't really matter."
> —Tucker Elliot, *The Rainy Season*

MOT

Ministry of Transport. Widely used in reference to the inspection certificate that all vehicles over a certain age must obtain in order to show that they have passed the safety and environmental tests established by the government. "My car's up for its MOT next week—could be an expensive job!"

MOTORWAY

A multi-lane freeway.

NUMBER PLATE

Plate that displays the registration number, required on all vehicles. It always remains with a car, even with change of ownership. Yellow in the rear and white on the front of the car.

OVERTAKE

To pass another vehicle. In the UK, this happens on the right.

PEDESTRIAN CROSSING

A crosswalk. The designated place for pedestrians to cross the street, indicated by stripes on the road surface. See **Zebra crossing** page 114 and **Belisha beacons** page 95.

PEDESTRIAN ISLAND

A small concrete island in the middle of the road, with lights at each end to which a pedestrian can run halfway across the road and then wait for the other side to clear.

PELICAN CROSSING

The name given to pedestrian a crossing that uses traffic lights to control motorized traffic. "Pelican" is an acronym derived from the name given to the crossings when they were first introduced in the 1960s: Pedestrian Light Controlled Crossing.

PETROL

Gasoline. Always sold by the liter.

PLATFORM

The place in a train station where passengers board and exit trains.

PRANG

A knock or crash. When applied to automobiles, Americans call this a "fender bender." Also a verb.

RELIANT ROBIN

A funny three-wheeled car. It is no longer made, but the term has entered British folklore for its amazing maneuverability.

RESIDENTS' PARKING

Certain areas of a street or neighborhood may be set aside and reserved for the parking of the residents who live there. Each of them will have purchased, at great expense, a permit allowing their vehicle to be in one of the residents' parking spots. Non-residents who park in these spots are risking a hefty fine.

RETURN TICKET

A ticket for a round-trip.

RING ROAD

An outer belt road around an urban area, also known as a "beltway" in the USA. See **Circular road** page 99.

ROUNDABOUT

A traffic circle of varying size, from a mile in diameter to as small as a few meters. A car always yields to the right. Most roundabouts are efficient and easy to navigate, but see **Gyratory system** page 101 and **Magic roundabout** page 105.

SENIOR RAIL CARD

A travel card for people over age sixty that, for an annual charge, gives a thirty percent discount on all rail fares throughout the UK. There are some restrictions.

SERVICES

An area off a motorway or "A" road where drivers can buy gas and food and use restrooms. Some locations have hotels. Garage or car-repair services are usually not available.

SHIPPING FORECAST

Broadcast on BBC Radio four times a day, this service provides updates on weather conditions for the seas and coastlines around the British Isles.

SINGLE TICKET

A one-way ticket.

SINGLE YELLOW

A yellow line of paint along the side of the road, indicating that parking is only allowed at specified times. See **Double yellow** page 100.

TAILBACK

A traffic jam.

TAX DISC

A small round disc issued by the government and displayed on the windshield of all autos showing that the bearer has paid the annual road tax. Although discontinued in 2015, the term is still widely used.

TFL

Transport for London, a governmental body responsible for
the London Underground, London Overground, Docklands
Light Railway, TfL Rail, roads, buses, taxis, river services,
cycle networks, local rail, and trams. Generally, if it moves
in London, it's administered by the TfL.

THREE-POINT TURN

An insane, yet legal, practice of turning around a vehicle
in the middle of a street despite oncoming traffic and the
resulting delays. Along with reversing around corners, it
was an integral part of the British driving test for decades.
In the driving test, it was officially called a "turn in the
road." If the road was very narrow, you could do a five-point
turn and still pass—as long as you were driving sensibly
and safely! Both maneuvers were dropped from the test in
2017 and replaced with new essential skills such as using
satellite navigation.

TRAFFIC CALMING

Yet another one of those insane ideas or philosophies that
make you wonder who thought it up. This idea is that by
introducing speed bumps (sleeping policemen) or one-way
islands, traffic will somehow be controlled, slowed down,
and overall calmer. It only serves to irritate everyone and
cause delays.

TRAIN GUARD

A conductor, often also the "ticket collector" and "checker." In addition to answering passenger questions and checking tickets, train guards are trained in operational safety and route knowledge. They are able to secure doors safely, protect the train, and act in emergencies like derailments or fires. The advent of automated ticket barriers is beginning to render this job obsolete.

TROLLEY DOLLY

Slang for a flight attendant.

TYRE

A tire.

ULTRA-LOW EMISSION ZONE (ULEZ)

A scheme introduced across Greater London in 2019 to try to reduce air pollution by imposing fines on the most polluting large vehicles. It has lower emission standards than the Low Emission Zone (LEZ). The ULEZ now operates twenty-four hours a day, seven days a week, every day of the year, within the same area of Central London where the Congestion Charge is imposed.

UNDERGROUND

The London Underground transport system. See **Tube** page 268.

> "The London Underground is not a political movement."
> —Jamie Lee Curtis as Wanda in *A Fish Called Wanda*

UNDERTAKE

To illegally pass another vehicle on the left on a multilane road.

VARIABLE SPEED LIMIT

A motorway speed limit that can be changed to suit traffic conditions, controlled by electronic matrix signs and legally enforceable. It is successfully used to reduce congestion by reducing the gaps between vehicles and regulating the flow of traffic.

WHEEL CLAMP

A device, usually yellow, that immobilizes the wheel of an illegally parked car. Often called a "boot" or a "Denver boot" in the USA.

WHITE VAN MEN

A UK stereotype describing tradesmen (e.g., electricians, builders, painters, decorators, or plumbers) who drive white vans for work. They are seen to be selfish, aggressive, and inconsiderate drivers and typically to be white, heterosexual, and fond of their cigarettes and beer.

WINDSCREEN

The windshield of a car.

ZEBRA CROSSING

A white-striped pedestrian road crossing with flashing yellow globe lights called "Belisha beacons." They are named for the zebra-like black and white stripes painted across the road. The pedestrian has priority on a zebra (pronounced "ZEBB-ra") crossing but should wait for the traffic to stop first before they set off. A zebra crossing is famously immortalized on the Abbey Road album cover. See **Belisha beacon** page 95.

7.

The Education System

THE BRITISH EDUCATION SYSTEM IS A SOURCE OF MORE THAN a little confusion, even within the British education system. Public schools versus private schools (not as obvious a distinction as you might think), GCSE exams, and a different meaning of "college" all cause Americans to scratch their heads. Assessment ideology, classroom decorum, funding, and government involvement in the education process are all different from their counterparts in American systems. Here is a very brief overview.

The education system in the UK is divided into four main parts: primary education, secondary education, further education, and higher education. Primary education begins in the UK at age five and continues until age eleven. From age eleven to age sixteen, students enter secondary school and start their work toward taking exams called "GCSEs." Although primary and secondary education are mandatory in Scotland, Wales, and Northern Ireland, education is optional after age sixteen. In England, a student must either remain in education until age eighteen or start an apprenticeship or traineeship. Scotland, Wales, and Northern Ireland each have different but similar rules.

Once students finish secondary education, they have the option to continue into further education to take exams called "A-Levels," "GNVQs," "BTECs," or "T-Levels." (See below for details.) British students who are planning to go to college or university are required to complete further education.

In England and Wales, the government introduced a National Curriculum in 1988. It provides a consistent instructional framework across all geographic regions for students between the ages of five and eighteen. All state schools are required to follow it. Independent schools are not required to follow the National Curriculum in every detail, but they must show that they provide a good all-round education. They are also inspected every few years.

A university undergraduate degree program takes three years in England,

A Lollipop Lady, page 104

Wales, and Northern Ireland. Scottish degree programs are similar to those in the USA and usually require four years of undergraduate study. An undergraduate degree may be a BA (Bachelor of Arts), BEng (Bachelor of Engineering), or BSc (Bachelor of Science). After earning a bachelor's degree, students may pursue master's degrees and PhDs.

11-PLUS

An optional examination taken during year six (sixth grade) to determine whether a child is capable of attending a selective secondary school or grammar school.

A-LEVELS

Standing for "Advanced Levels," these are courses intended to qualify students for university. Students take A-Levels during their first year of "sixth form" (ages seventeen and eighteen). Students may take anywhere from three to five A-Levels during the first year and three during their second year. A-Levels were introduced in 1951 and were designed to focus students on subjects that they might want to study in university. The system is similar to the Advanced Placement program in the USA.

AS-LEVEL

An AS-Level is considered equivalent to half an A-Level and can be done as a standalone qualification or as the first half of a full A-Level. It works like a GCSE in that it consists of course work and a final exam and is in an individual subject, but it is considerably harder and more academic. It is designed to guide a student toward university.

"Intelligence was a deformity which must be concealed; a public school taught one to conceal it as a good tailor hides a paunch or a hump."

—Cyril Connolly

117

BIRO

>A ballpoint pen; invented by the Hungarian Laszlo Jozsef Biro in the 1940s. This brand name has now become a generic word for a ballpoint pen. (Prounounced "BUY-ro.")

BTEC

>"BTEC" stands for the "Business and Technology Education Council." This became a part the exam board Edexcel, which was acquired by the educational publishing company Pearson plc in 2013. Its name lives on in a series of vocational tests validated and offered by Pearson. BTECs are specialized, work-related exams. They are designed for students who are interested in a particular sector of industry but not yet sure what job they'd like to do. Students can study BTECs alongside (or instead of) GCSEs and A-Levels in schools and colleges.

CITY & GUILDS

>A broad range of vocational tests offered by the City & Guilds of London Institute, an examining and accreditation body for work-related training in the UK. These exams are not generally used to meet university entrance requirements.

CLEARING

>If a UCAS (Universities and Colleges Admissions Service) undergraduate application is unsuccessful, then "Clearing" is another UCAS service a student can use to look for alternative courses. Whether a student didn't receive offers, declined offers, or didn't get the grades needed for

acceptance, clearing allows him or her to apply for courses that still have vacancies shortly before the start of the academic year. The process begins in mid-August each year. See **UCAS** page 126.

COLLEGE

A place that traditionally gave students qualifications below the level of a university degree, often in the skills they needed to do a particular job. However, in recent years many colleges in the UK have formed partnerships with British universities to offer "top-up" courses that allow a student to continue to a full degree at the college. About ten percent of all undergraduate higher education is delivered in "further education" (FE) colleges. A few universities, most famously Oxford and Cambridge, have entities within them that are also called "colleges." At these universities, the colleges are independent and self-governing. The university acts as a central governing system.

DRAWING PINS

Push pins or thumb tacks.

EXTERNAL EXAMINER

An academic from an outside institution who checks grading and degree awards in consultation with the institution's own examination board.

FOUNDATION DEGREE

A university-level vocational course equal to the first two years of a three-year bachelor's degree course. Taking two years full-time (there are also part-time programs of varying lengths), it is possible to then progress to a linked degree course upon completion, with the award of a full honors degree after a further year of study.

FRESHERS' WEEK

An orientation week for new university or college students.

GCSE

British educational exams that schoolchildren take when they are fourteen to sixteen years old. "GCSE" is an abbreviation for "General Certificate of Secondary Education." GCSEs were introduced in 1986, replacing the previous O-Level and CSE systems.

GNVQ

An acronym for "General National Vocational Qualification," a certificate of competence in a trade. These have been phased out in recent years, and the last GNVQs were awarded in 2007.

> "Grammar schools are public schools without the sodomy."
> —Tony Parsons

GRAMMAR SCHOOL

This is an educational institution in England that is gradually being phased out but is still present in some areas. Entrance to these government-funded secondary schools is by way of an examination called the "11-plus" entrance exam that children take when they are age eleven or twelve. Those who do well on the exam can go on to grammar schools for a rigorous university-preparation curriculum. Since the late 1970s, students have been admitted without examination into modern comprehensive secondary schools that accept students with all levels of abilities. No new grammar schools may be established, but those already in existence have been allowed to continue in operation.

HEADMASTER/HEADMISTRESS

The school principal.

> "The only real drawback of the school was the fact that the headmaster happened to be a sadist."
>
> —Lord Berners

HIGHER NATIONAL CERTIFICATE (HNC)

This is a vocationally focused credential. It's earned through a work-based course that usually takes one year to complete. Roughly equivalent to one year of university study.

HND

Higher national diplomas (HNDs) are earned through a work-based course that is equal to two years at university. It can lead straight into a career or be "topped up" by further study to become a full bachelor's degree. Full-time HNDs take around two years to complete.

HOP THE WAG

To play hooky; skip school.

MARKING

Grading, assessment of a student's work.

MARKS

Grades.

> "He shows great originality, which must be curbed at all cost."
> —Peter Ustinov's school report card

MASTER/MISTRESS

An old-fashioned and formal title for a teacher of a specific subject. "He was my history master at school." "She is the games mistress."

MUCKING ABOUT

Fooling around, as in "mucking about like a group of schoolboys."

NATIONAL CURRICULUM

The National Curriculum is a set of subjects and standards used by primary and secondary schools, so children across the land learn the same things. It covers what subjects are taught and the standards that children should reach in each subject.

OFQUAL

The Office of Qualifications and Examinations Regulation. It regulates the following qualifications, examinations, and assessments in England:
- GCSEs
- A-Levels
- AS-Levels
- Vocational and technical qualifications

O-LEVELS

Short for "ordinary level," the O-Level used to be the first level of standard educational examinations in specific subjects taken by British students. They were replaced by the GCSE in 1987 but are still widely used in conversation.

ORDINARY DEGREE

A degree passed without honors. Some universities offer ordinary degree courses in their own right. Ordinary degrees can also be awarded to those students who do complete an honors degree course, but without achieving the conditions required to gain "honours."

PGCE

A PGCE is a post-graduate certificate in education that combines student teaching with education theory. Types of

PGCEs include early years, primary, secondary, and further education. PGCEs can be completed in just nine months.

> "The only time my education was interrupted was when I was at school."
> —George Bernard Shaw

PUBLIC SCHOOL

Contrary to what you might guess, you must pay to attend a public school. It actually is a private school. The most famous examples include Eton and Harrow. When I first moved to the UK, and people referred to politicians as "public schoolboys," I thought they were being derogatory. Later, I discovered that they *were* being derogatory!

> "A public schoolboy must be acceptable at a dance and invaluable in a shipwreck."
> —Alan Bennett

NATIONAL QUALIFICATIONS FRAMEWORK (NQF)

Since 2015, all qualifications in the UK have been governed by a "framework" that defines, standardizes, and links the many levels of study and credit values of different educational programs.

RESIT

To retake an examination, usually because of failure or getting a low grade on the previous examination.

SCHOOL DINNER

    Hot lunch served at school.

SIXTH FORM

    An option in the education systems of England, Northern Ireland, and Wales, sixth form consists of two years of full-time education taken after GCSE level. Sixth-form students (typically between sixteen and eighteen years of age) prepare for their A-Level (or equivalent) examinations. "I met my lifelong friend while we were at sixth form together."

STATE SCHOOL

    A school open to the public without charge.

T-LEVELS

    T-Levels are new courses started in September of 2020, which follow GCSEs and are equivalent to three A-Levels. These two-year courses were developed in collaboration with employers and businesses to ensure that the content meets the needs of industry and prepares students for work. T-Levels offer students a mixture of classroom learning and on-the-job experience.

125

UCAS

The Universities and Colleges Admissions Service. This independent body receives and processes all applications to all universities in the UK. Applications are subsequently presented to the student's first, second, and third university of choice, and an acceptance decision is made. See **Clearing** page 118.

8.

Cooking and Foods

THE REPUTATION OF POOR AND BLAND FOOD IN THE UK IS undeserved today, and yet it hangs around in American popular culture like the smell of cooking cabbage. The image of the Brit abroad as an unadventurous eater is also inaccurate but still serves as humorous fodder for the makers of television shows and cinema. It is true that even today there remains some residue of a rationing mentality among those who lived through WWII and the post-war shortages. Portions are modest, and leftovers are saved for tomorrow.

In recent decades, the influence of the European Union and the resulting freedom of movement, the increased availability of fresh produce and meat, improved cultural awareness and, in no small part, the advent of the "gastro-pub" have altered British perceptions of what constitutes good food. Good wine is readily available, and there is no better Indian cuisine in the world. (Yes, I said *the world*.) Nonetheless, the British kitchen, British cooking, dining out, and the grocery store remain minefields of misunderstanding for the American visitor.

127

You will no doubt notice the plethora of "biscuits" in the list below. The British are mad for their biscuits, and this strikes many Americans as a bit eccentric until they learn that a biscuit is a cookie, and they try one with a good cup of tea. Suddenly it all becomes clear!

AFTERNOON TEA

Introduced in the early 1800s, this was a small meal to stave off hunger until a larger and later evening meal. Originally this consisted of small sandwiches cut into "fingers" and cakes. The scones we all associate with afternoon tea were not introduced until the early twentieth century.

AFTERS

Dessert, as in "What's for afters?" If you're upper class ("posh"), you'll call the dish at the end of the meal "pudding," irrespective of the actual nature of the food. So, yes, even some fancy concoction of cream and chocolate would be "pudding." "Sweet" is another tern for dessert, but this might signify that you come from the other end of the social spectrum.

ARBROATH SMOKIE

A type of Scandinavian dark smoked haddock—a specialty of the town of Arbroath on the east coast of Scotland. At first, these may seem inedible, but the taste grows on you.

These can be bought along the roadside near Arbroath and in most shops in town.

AUBERGINE

Eggplant.

BACON

English bacon is different from American bacon. In the USA, bacon has a fairly consistent and singular definition. American bacon is streaky with fat, because it comes from pork belly, one of the fattiest parts of the pig. English bacon, on the other hand, is cut from the loin, located in the middle of the pig's back, where the meat is leaner, thicker, and chewier. It is sold as "back bacon" or "streaky bacon." English bacon can be smoked or unsmoked, and slices are all referred to as "rashers," irrespective of type. Some Brits like it cooked crisp, some like it served less well done. If you order bacon in a restaurant, you're likely to be served back bacon. It won't be crisp unless you request it that way, and even if you do, your request may be declined.

> "I would walk miles for a bacon sandwich."
> — Diana, Princess of Wales

BANGERS

Sausages. The story goes that after World War II, sausages contained so much water that they often exploded during the cooking process. The term may also refer to an old, beat-up automobile.

BAP

Bread roll. The actual origins of the term "bap" remain unknown, although the first evidence of the word in relation to bread came in the sixteenth century. The term is used in many different areas of Britain, including most of Scotland and Northern Ireland as well as areas of London and parts of the North of England. See **Bread roll** page 133.

BARM, BARM CAKE

The word for a bread roll used by people in the northwest of England, including Manchester. The term derives from the use of barm—the foam on top of beer—to help bread rise. In the town of Wigan, a meat-and-potato pie sandwiched inside a barm cake is known as a "Wigan Kebab." See **Bread roll** page 133.

BATCH

Bread roll. The word is rare, although it is the term of choice in both Coventry and Nuneaton. The origins of the word are uncertain, although some think that it evolved from the middle English word "bache," which meant to bake. See **Bread roll** page 133.

BEETROOT

Beet.

BHARJI, BHAJI

A small piece of Indian food made of vegetables, flour, egg, and water, formed into a golf-ball-sized sphere and deep fried. Try onion or cauliflower bharji in an Indian restaurant—delicious! (Not to be confused with "bargy.")

> "As an American, I classify *I'm a Celebrity, Get me out of Here* in the category of impenetrable British mysteries—like beans on toast."
>
> —Molly Ivins

BISCUITS

Cookies, not American-style biscuits. British biscuits are a hard, sweet baked snack that may have fruit in them or be topped with chocolate. They are frequently eaten dunked in a "cuppa" tea. In the grocery or market, you'll find a dizzying selection of biscuits. Here are some to try, if only for their appealing names:

- Battenberg
- Dundee Cake
- Eccles Cake
- French Fancies
- Victoria Sandwich

BLACK PUDDING

A type of blood sausage, usually very dark in color. It has a black skin and is made from pork fat or beef suet, pig's blood, and a cereal like barley or oatmeal. Traditionally served with a "full English" breakfast, it remains fairly popular in parts of England and Scotland..

BLACK TREACLE

Molasses, sometimes referred to as just "treacle."

BOURBON (BISCUIT)

A sandwich-style cookie consisting of two thin rectangular chocolate-flavored biscuits with a chocolate buttercream filling.

BOVRIL

The trade name of a thick, dark brown, salty beef extract made into a drink by diluting it with hot water. Originally created in 1871 for Napoleon's army, it is sold today in a distinctive, bulbous, dark brown jar. It is also used to flavor soups or stews or to spread on toast. You can even get Bovril-flavored potato chips. Bovril is also popular in Malaysia, Singapore, and China, where generations of people have grown up with this iconic British drink.

BRANSTON PICKLE

A brown, vinegar-based brand-name preserve of diced cucumber, onion, and spices. Very tasty but strong. Often served with a strong cheddar cheese and bread as part of a "ploughman's lunch."

BREAD CAKE

See **Bread roll** page 133.

BREAD ROLL

A word someone uses to define a plain, roll-shaped piece of bread used to create a sandwich varies, depending on which part of the country you're in. This has led to continuing debate about what is the "right" name for a ball of bread. Terms include:

- Barm or barm cake, used in northern England
- Bap, used in Scotland and Northern Ireland
- Batch, used in Coventry
- Bin lid, used in Liverpool
- Bread cake, used in Yorkshire
- Bun, used generally in northern England
- Buttery, used in Scotland
- Cob, used in the English Midlands
- Morning roll, in general use
- Muffin, used in West Manchester and Northern Ireland
- Nudger, used in Liverpool
- Oven bottom, used in Lancashire
- Roll, recognized nationally
- Rowies, used in Wales
- Stottie cake (or Stotty), used in northeastern England
- Teacake, used in Yorkshire

> An American colleague at the American College in London was in her first week on the job. Traditionally, in the mornings, someone made a breakfast run across the street to the local bakery. As a prank, one day she was asked to go and collect a dozen loo rolls. She dutifully went and asked the baker.
>
> —M.H.

BRIDIE

A hand-held Scottish meat pastry filled with chopped steak, butter, and beef suet. See **Cornish pasty** page 137 and **Oggie** page 152.

BROAD BEANS

Fava beans. Flat, round beans that are light green in color. These must be shelled like peas to harvest the beans inside the pods. Not to be confused with French beans, which are what Americans call "green beans."

BROWN SAUCE

A generic term for a tart sauce used as a condiment with hot and cold savory food and as an ingredient in soups and stews. The most popular brand is HP Sauce, which has a tomato base blended with malt vinegar and tamarind.

> "Only a nation that thought of food as an extension of engineering would have invented brown sauce. You can clean silver with it. It doesn't go with anything. It's a culinary assassin, an olfactory blackout. And it's got tamarinds in it. "Ere Guv, we've got these weird little fruits from out east. What will we do with them?' 'Chuck them in the brown sauce.'"
>
> —A.A. Gill

BUBBLE AND SQUEAK

A delicious concoction of fried mashed potato and cabbage, often made from leftovers. Named for the bubbling and squeaking that occurs while it's being cooked. Originally the dish contained meat, but that fell out of the recipe during the rationing period after World War II. The first known reference to the term dates to 1770.

BUCK'S FIZZ

Mimosa. A drink made by mixing champagne and orange juice. Also a musical group that represented the UK in the Eurovision song contest in 1981 ... and won!

BUN

A bread roll. Used commonly in northeastern England, southern Wales, and much of Northern Ireland. A bun used to mean a sweeter roll enhanced with butter, like a French brioche, but over time it has come to mean any small bread roll. See **Bread roll** page 133.

BUTTY

A sandwich, as in "I'll have a bacon butty." Particularly used from Birmingham northward. See **Sarnie** page 156.

CAFÉ

A staple of British culture, a café (sometimes pronounced "caf") is an eatery that is popular with diners who are in a hurry. They provide take-out food and are famous for bap sandwiches and "full English breakfast." Cafés open early and are never open in the evening. See **English breakfast** page 141.

CANDY FLOSS

Cotton candy.

CAULIFLOWER CHEESE

A traditional British baked dish of cauliflower covered in a creamy cheese sauce with a dash of Dijon mustard. It is considered children's food, but adults love it, too. It can also be made with broccoli, but then it is (unsurprisingly) called "broccoli cheese." Real comfort food.

CHIPS

French fries or deep-fried potato wedges. The British version is generally a bit larger than the French fry. They are not American potato chips, which are called "crisps" in the UK.

> "The English contribution to world cuisine—the chip."
> —Kevin Kline as Otto in *A Fish Called Wanda*

COB

This is the word for a bread roll used by people in the English Midlands, especially in cities in the east, such as Nottingham. The exact origins of the word are not known, although some people say that the word originated from the word "cop," which means head. Others think the word came from people saying that they looked like a cobblestone or cob. See **Bread roll** page 133.

COCK-A-LEEKIE SOUP

>A Scottish soup made of leeks and peppered chicken stock. Often thickened with rice or sometimes barley.

CORN

>Grain. Any kind of grain. It does not mean corn in the American sense. In the UK, corn—as in corn on the cob—is called "maize."

CORN FLOUR

>Corn starch. *Not* corn meal or polenta!

> "Good apple pies are a considerable part of our domestic happiness."
>
> —Jane Austen

CORNISH PASTY

>A hand-held savory pie filled with meat and vegetables, often beef and rutabaga. See **Bridie** page 134 and **Oggie** page 152.

CORIANDER

>Cilantro. What Americans call "coriander," the British call "coriander seeds."

COURGETTE

>Zucchini. (Pronounced cor-ZHET.)

CREAM CRACKER

A cracker that is similar to a saltine but bigger and not sprinkled with salt.

CREAM TEA

A light—well, fairly light—snack traditionally enjoyed in the mid-afternoon. It consists of scones with jam and clotted cream accompanied by a cup of tea. While readily available everywhere, the cream tea is a specialty of England's West Country and the subject of fierce debate. In Devon, the cream is spread first, then topped with jam, while in Cornwall the tradition is jam first, cream second. My suggestion is to try it both ways and make up your own mind!

CRISPS

Potato chips.

CUP OF CHAR

Cup of tea. "Char" might be an anglicization of the Indian word "cha" or "chai" but could also stem from the Chinese "tcha."

CUPPA

A cup of tea. "Let's sit down, have a cuppa, and talk about it."

CURRANT (BLACK AND RED)

A woody shrub grown in the UK for its red or black berries. Black currants are used in producing Ribena, a popular brand of soft drink concentrate. The taste is sharp but sweet.

CURRY

Officially, curry is the blend of spices and herbs used in Indian cooking. However, the word has become widely used to describe Indian cooking generally, such as "Shall we go out for a curry?" Curry was recently voted England's second-favorite take-out dish. (Chinese was first.)

CUSTARD

A sweet yellow dessert made from milk, eggs, and sugar. It is often served with fruits and puddings. There are also powdered custard mixes, the most popular being Bird's Custard Powder. See **Trifle** page 163.

CUSTARD CREAM BISCUIT

A popular sandwich-style cookie often served in the afternoon with a cup of tea. Traditionally, they have a buttery vanilla flavor, but there are other varieties, including coconut, chocolate, and citrus.

DESICCATED COCONUT

Shredded and dried coconut meat.

DIGESTIVE BISCUIT

A round, semisweet cookie made from whole meal flour, similar to graham crackers. Although they were originally developed to aid digestion, it's generally accepted now that this claim is unfounded. They're also are available with a chocolate coating on one side.

DINNER

Well this is obvious, isn't it? It's the evening meal. Well, yes and no. This depends on your age, geographical location, and social standing. For most people in the UK, the three meals of the day are breakfast, lunch, and dinner. In years past, however, children had dinnertime at school, and tea in the evening. In many parts of northern England, these terms still apply—the three standard meals there are breakfast, dinner, and tea. And then there's another term, "supper." To many in the UK, this means a fourth meal or a snack—cheese on toast maybe—if needed before bed. But in some cases, "supper" is used to describe the main evening meal, just as it is in the USA. So, if you're ever invited to someone's house for supper, you can pretty much assume it'll be a full dinner and not a slice of cheese before beddy-bye!

EGGY BREAD

French toast.

"English children are still raised to enjoy a range of foodstuffs that are more or less inedible. These include such offerings as the chip butty (French fries between slices of white bread) and perplexing toppings for toast, like canned spaghetti and baked beans and Marmite, a black, salty, yeasty spread that causes gagging in foreign nationals."

—Rebecca Mead

ELEVENSES

A tea and biscuit (cookie) break customarily taken around eleven a.m.

ENDIVE

Chicory.

ENGLISH BREAKFAST

Sometimes called a "fry up," a full English breakfast consists of two eggs, bacon, toast, sausage, a fried tomato, black pudding, mushrooms, and tea. Variations include baked beans, English chips, and fried bread. See **Bacon** page 129.

FAGGOT

This really threw me when I first arrived in the UK. One meaning of "faggot" is low-quality minced pork formed into meatballs. "Faggot" is also sometimes used as a term for a group of twigs or sticks tied together to light a fire. It is historically associated with burning at the stake.

FAIRY CAKE

A cupcake.

FAYRE

An old-fashioned spelling of "fare," used to describe the type of food available on a menu.

FISH FINGERS

Fish sticks. Usually made from cod, but many other varieties are available.

> "A good fish finger butty is hard to beat."
>
> —Jamie Oliver

FLAPJACKS

Oat bars—sometimes with the addition of nuts or dried fruits. The oats are mixed with butter and golden syrup and baked. Once cool, they are cut into squares. Not American pancakes, English flapjacks are more like cookies and eaten as a snack.

FLOUR

In the UK, one can purchase plain flour and self-raising flour. In the USA, flour choices include all-purpose flour, pastry flour, cake flour, and self-rising flour. While they both contain baking powder, UK self-*raising* flour is not identical to American self-*rising* flour, so watch out!

FRENCH BEANS

Green beans.

FRENCH LOAF

A generic term referring to any French bread but usually associated with a baguette. It is also known as a "French stick."

FULL ENGLISH

See **English breakfast** page 141.

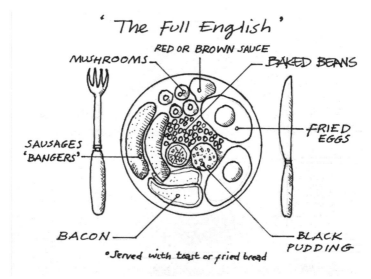

'The Full English'

MUSHROOMS — RED OR BROWN SAUCE — BAKED BEANS — FRIED EGGS — SAUSAGES 'BANGERS' — BACON — BLACK PUDDING

• Served with toast or fried bread

> "Tourists tend to enjoy the traditional English breakfasts because they don't eat such things often at home. If they did, they would die."
>
> —Lonely Planet's *Great Britain*

GARIBALDI BISCUIT

A classic British cookie named after the nineteenth-century Italian general. They have a black currant filling that has given rise to some unappetizing but descriptive nicknames, including: "squashed fly biscuits," "dead fly biscuits," "flies' graveyards," and "fly sandwiches."

GOLDEN SYRUP

Light-colored golden treacle produced by the evaporation of cane sugar juice. Originally a by-product of the sugar-refining process developed by Tate & Lyle at the end of the nineteenth century. Golden syrup looks like honey and is sometimes used as a honey alternative. Used to sweeten and flavor cakes and puddings.

My first trip to a supermarket in the UK was a baffling experience. In addition to all the foods that I didn't recognize, there were items in the freezer cabinet which made me gasp. In addition to "spotted dick," there was "toad in the hole." I couldn't help but wonder what kind of a country I'd moved to.
—M.H.

GOOSEBERRY

A small green fruit that grows on low bushes and has tiny hairs. There are many varieties, and most have a very sharp, sour taste. Used for making pies and jams.

GRILL (OVEN)

To broil.

"We English don't have a lot to be proud of, but we can be proud of our mustard. On the continent, mustard is used to bring out the flavour of meat, but English mustard really makes your nose bleed."

—Jack Dee

HAGGIS

A traditional Scottish food, haggis is a large sausage, usually shaped like a ball, which is made from minced sheep organ meat (heart, liver, and lungs), onion, oatmeal, suet, and spices, all contained inside a sheep's stomach. Haggis is traditionally made and eaten during Burns Night celebrations.

HARICOT BEANS

Navy beans. (Pronounced "HARRY-co.")

HERBS

This has the same meaning as in the USA, but the initial "h" is pronounced. In the UK, pronouncing it without the "h" on the front sounds pretentious or—Heaven forbid!—like you're trying to be French. "Herb" is also a Rastafarian term meaning ganja/weed/marijuana.

HOBNOBS

Delicious, rustic, oat-based cookies. A milk chocolate variant was introduced in 1987. Perfect with a cup of tea, the Hobnob is the third-most popular cookie in the UK. The name "Hobnob" comes from Shakespeare's *Twelfth Night*.

HP SAUCE

Omnipresent in the UK, this tart brand of sauce is used as a condiment with hot and cold savory food and as an ingredient in soups and stews. Also known generically as just "brown sauce," it has a tomato base blended with malt vinegar and tamarind. The HP reputedly stands for "Houses of Parliament."

HUNDREDS AND THOUSANDS

Sprinkles (for ice cream or cakes).

ICE LOLLY

A popsicle.

ICING SUGAR

Powdered sugar, confectioner's sugar.

JACKET POTATO

A baked potato. These are a staple of cafés, usually offered with a selection of toppings, including tuna, sweet corn, baked beans, cheese, and sometimes all of the above

JAFFA CAKES

Small cookies with a layer of sponge cake topped with sweet orange jam and finished off with semi-sweet chocolate. Named after Jaffa oranges, Jaffa Cakes are so loved in the UK that they've been ranked the bestselling biscuit.

> "I'm half British, half American. My passport has an eagle with a teabag in its beak."
>
> —Bob Hope

JAM

A clear or translucent fruit spread that Americans call "jelly." See **Jelly** below.

JAM ROLY-POLY

A favorite children's desert made from suet dough, spread with jam and then rolled up. Originally, it was boiled in muslin fabric, but these days it's steamed or baked. It can also be filled with golden syrup, apples, or prunes.

JELLY

Jell-O. Flavored gelatin, not what Americans call "jelly."

JOINT

A piece of meat prepared for Sunday lunch. Can also mean a body part or marijuana cigarette.

KIPPER

A small, oily fish, usually herring, which has been split, preserved in salt, and then smoked. It is often eaten for breakfast.

LARDY CAKE

A traditional rich, sweet bread eaten for special occasions and holidays. The main ingredients are lard, flour, sugar, spices, currants, and raisins. It is most often eaten with tea or coffee in the afternoon.

LIQUOR

Liquor is a savory parsley sauce commonly served with traditional London-style pie and mash. The word "liquor" also refers to any liquid in which something has been cooked. It can also refer to alcoholic drinks, but it's less commonly used in the UK than in the USA. (In the UK, the more common term is "spirits.")

MAIN COURSE

An entrée. This is confusing to Americans, because in the UK, "entrée" means "first course." The "first course" is sometimes known as a "starter" or "hors d'oeuvre."

MANGE TOUT

Snow pea. This means "eat everything" in French. Applied to these peas because you eat them pod and all.

MAIN COURSE

An entrée. This is confusing to Americans, because in the UK, "entrée" means "first course." The "first course" is sometimes known as a "starter" or "hors d'oeuvre."

MAIZE

Corn. American-style corn, as in "corn on the cob."

MARMITE

A brand name of a paste made from yeast extract. A by-product of beer brewing, it has a yeasty, salty, soy saucy flavor. Its ability to inspire strong reactions inspired a marketing slogan: "Love it or hate it." Marmite has infiltrated British culture and language to the point where anyone or anything that defies indifference can be described as being "like Marmite."

MEASURES

I once attempted to bake a cake on "gas mark 9" and burned it to a crisp, primarily because I had no idea what a gas mark was. Cooking became only slightly more possible once I printed out the differences between American and British standard measurements. Here's an overview:

- Oven temperature is measured in gas marks. The most commonly used is gas mark 5, which equals 375 degrees Fahrenheit.

British Gas Mark	Fahrenheit
1	275°F
2	300°F
3	325°F
4	350°F
5	375°F
6	400°F
7	425°F
8	450°F
9	475°F

- Weights are measured in grams. American recipes sometimes confusingly call for ingredients by volume, but these commodities may only be sold in the UK by weight. For example, one cup of sugar is 225 grams, but also about 240 milliliters.

British	American
15g	½ oz
30g	1 oz
110g	4 oz
225g	8 oz
450g	1 lb

• Liquid volumes are measured in milliliters. One American cup is equal to about 250 ml. One US teaspoon is equal to about 5 milliliters. What you won't find in any recipe in the UK is mention of "cup" measurement. There is no such valuation in British cooking.

Milliliters	British	American
3.55 ml	1 UK teaspoon	0.72 US teaspoon
5 ml	1.5 UK teaspoon	1 US teaspoon
15 ml	1 UK tablespoon	1 US tablespoon
60 ml	4.25 UK tablespoons	1/4 US cup
80 ml	6 UK tablespoons	1/3 US cup
125 ml	9 UK tablespoons	1/2 US cup
250 ml	18 UK tablespoons	1 US cup
4.73 ml	0.83 UK pint	1 US pint
500 ml	0.88 UK pint	2 US cups
570 ml	1 UK pint	2.40 US cups
948 ml	1.67 UK pints	4 US cups
1 liter	1.75 UK pints	2.11 US pints
2 liters	3.5 UK pints	4.23 US pints
3.79 liters	0.83 UK gallon	1 US gallon
6.8 liters	1.25 UK gallon	1.5 US gallon
7.57 liters	1.67 UK gallon	2 US gallons

MINCE

Ground meat, as in ground beef or lamb. It means minced meat, but not mincemeat—see the next entry.

MINCEMEAT

A mixture of dried fruit, spices, and suet. Historically, it did once contain meat. It's now used mainly as a filling for delicious small pies, traditionally at Christmas time.

MUFFIN

Unlike American muffins, these bread rolls are not sweet. See **Oven bottom** page 153.

MUSHY PEAS

Cooked and mashed green peas served with fish and chips, especially in northern England. An acquired taste.

NEEPS

Diced rutabaga. When served with potatoes, they're called "neeps and tatties." A term of Scottish origin.

OFF

Spoiled or rotten. "The milk has gone off."

OGGIE

A savory handheld pie with a buttery crust and rich, meaty filling, made of lamb and leeks. Oggies were traditionally eaten by miners for lunch down in the mines. See **Cornish pasty** page 137 and **Bridie** page 134.

OK SAUCE

A brand of brown sauce once considered rather old-fashioned—and therefore rarely found on supermarket shelves—but once again selling in volume because of its popularity in the Chinese community. It's often provided as a condiment option in Chinese restaurants.

OREGANO

Oregano, the Mediterranean herb used in cooking, but note the British pronunciation: "o-reh-GAH-no."

OVEN BOTTOM

A bread roll. This term is used in Lancashire and parts of Yorkshire. Before ovens with shelves became commonplace toward the end of the nineteenth century, all baked goods were cooked on the oven bottom, so the term "oven bottom" is relatively recent. See **Bread roll** page 133.

PECKISH

A bit hungry. "I'm not starving, just a little peckish."

PICKLE

Branston's Pickle and generic versions. "Pickle" can also mean vegetables preserved in brine or vinegar with herbs and spices. The term can also be used to describe a difficult or confusing situation. "I'm really in a pickle here!"

PIE AND MASH

A savory pie and mashed potatoes. Pies have been a staple of the British diet for centuries. The pie-and-mash shops offer meals that are steeped in history and ingrained in the very fabric of the UK. The main dish is the pastry pie traditionally filled with eel or cheaper cuts of meat like ground beef and mutton. Chicken and vegetarian fillings are also now common. While pie and mash has humble origins, it's now back in style at some of London's trendy restaurants.

PIGS IN BLANKETS

Small sausages or wieners wrapped in bacon. Traditionally, these are served as an accompaniment to roast turkey at Christmas dinner.

PLOUGHMAN'S LUNCH

A midday meal of a large slice of cheddar cheese, served with bread and a healthy portion of pickled relish. Commonly served in pubs. Goes well with a pint!

PORK PIE

A freestanding—no pie pan needed!—savory pie with pork filling.

PRAWN

A shrimp. In the USA, the term "prawn" is used for large or freshwater shrimp, but in the UK the word is the general term for all shrimp.

PUDDING

Dessert. Sometimes called a "sweet." "Pudding" usually implies that the dish has been cooked. See **Spotted dick** page 158.

RAPESEED

Usually referred to as canola in the USA, although it is a member of the mustard family.

RASHER

A single slice of bacon. See **Bacon** page 129.

RIBENA

The brand name of a soft drink concentrate made from black currants.

ROAST DINNER

An English Sunday tradition of having roast beef, lamb, or chicken for a main meal. See **Sunday roast** page 160.

ROASTIES

Potatoes roasted in the oven in oil or goose fat and basted occasionally. This produces a crisp exterior. Delicious!

ROCKET

Arugula.

ROLLMOPS

A fillet of herring, sometimes salted or pickled, rolled around a savory filling like an onion. Scandinavian in origin, they are usually served as an hors d'oeuvre.

ROUND OF TOAST

A piece of toast.

RUNNER BEANS

A variety of string beans.

SACHET

A small packet of something, e.g., sugar or salt. (Pronounced SASH-ay.)

SARNIE, SANGER

A sandwich, as in "I'll 'ave a bacon sarnie, love!"

SAUSAGE ROLL

A traditional British savory snack made of puff pastry with sausage filling.

SCONE

Similar to an American biscuit. Served with jam and clotted cream, scones are an integral part of a "cream tea." (Doesn't quite rhyme with "cone," but it isn't quite "scawn," either. Go for something in between.)

SCOTCH EGG

A hard-boiled egg encased in sausage meat, breaded, and deep fried or baked. Commonly available in pubs and popular for picnics.

SCRUMMY

Delicious. "That Scotch egg looks scrummy!"

It took me a couple of summers to figure out the British picnic. It's quite unlike the organized American version. British picnics tend to be hurried and thrown-together affairs held spontaneously when the sun makes an appearance, and often the food is picked up from Marks & Spencer on the way. There are few designated picnic areas and no shelters. Picnics can be held anywhere, at a roadside rest stop, a community park, or just out in the countryside. I attended one picnic at a stony beach that involved a disposable grill. It had to be protected from the wind and rain by several umbrellas, ultimately a futile effort. We ended up in a pub.

—M.H.

SCRUMPING

Taking fruit from someone else's tree—usually apples—without permission.

SEMOLINA

Ground durum wheat. In the UK, this is usually made into a pudding with milk and served as a children's food.

SOLDIERS

Pieces of toast cut into strips and used to dip into a soft-boiled egg that has had the top part of its shell removed. So named because they are cut in straight pieces and lined up on a plate—like soldiers on parade.

SPOTTED DICK

Steamed sponge pudding speckled with dark dried currants or raisins. It is usually served with custard or with butter and brown sugar. "Dick" is an old word that possibly meant pudding, but there is no definite etymology. Delicious and also the source of endless jokes.

> "Spotted dick is not a venereal disease!"
> —Schoolyard joke that's been around forever.

STARTER

Appetizer or hors d'oeuvre. The first course of a dinner.

STICK OF ROCK

Candy sticks. Commonly sold at seaside tourist spots like Blackpool and Brighton.

STOTTIE (STOTTY)

A term for a bread roll favored by Yorkshire bread lovers and residents of northern England. Originally, the stottie cake was a flat, round loaf about twelve inches in diameter with an indentation in the center. Some bakeries still produce authentic stotties, but the word is now also used to describe a generic bread roll. See **Bread roll** page 133.

SULTANA

A golden raisin made from yellow sultana grapes. Sweeter and juicier than American raisins.

"As a measure of how British I have become over the last twenty years of living here, I've started to carry my own tea bags with me when I return to the States to visit family. You just cannot get good regular tea in America. They've got all that flavored stuff—strawberry, lemon, and jasmine nonsense. Once I went looking for PG Tips (a universally available British brand) in a Kroger's store and was somewhat befuddled to find them in the "foreign foods" section at a price four times what it should have been. At least I found them!

While I was stateside, I noticed products on sale as 'Genuine British,' which I had never seen in Britain. I think they just make stuff up and label it British. I do miss Oreos."
—Ashley Stevenson, expat

SUNDAY ROAST

Sunday dinner, a wonderful British tradition. The meal consists of roast beef, chicken, or lamb served with roast potatoes (roasties), Yorkshire pudding, and vegetables. These days, traditional country pubs serve Sunday roasts. The enduring popularity of the Sunday roast has saved many a pub from financial ruin.

SWEDE

A rutabaga. Swedes originally came from Sweden and were known as "Swedish turnips." This was eventually shortened to "swede."

SWEETS

Generic term for candy. The singular "sweet" usually refers to the dessert course at dinner.

SWISS ROLL

A jelly roll.

TAKEAWAY OR TAKEOUT

Takeout. Food prepared "to go." "Shall we get a takeaway tonight?"

TANDOORI

A style of Indian cuisine popular in the UK. The name comes from "tandoor," the traditional fired-clay oven used to prepare the food.

TARAMOSALATA

A pink-colored Greek dish made out of salted or cured fish eggs (cod, carp, or grey mullet) mixed with olive oil, lemon juice, and garlic. Usually served with pita bread as a dip or spread.

TART

A delicious pie-like dessert, and also a word for a woman. In the past, the term was affectionate rhyming slang for sweetheart—jam tart. It now usually means a prostitute or promiscuous woman. See **Slapper** page 76.

TATTIES

A Scottish term for potatoes, this word is now used informally in other parts of the UK.

TEA (DRINK)

Also known as "char," this beverage is served hot, usually with milk, and often with a lot of sugar. Tea is important to the British, and there are deeply held beliefs bordering on religious fervor about the way to make the perfect "cuppa." Does the milk go into the cup first, or the tea? How long to let it brew before it "stews?" The answers to these questions are debated perennially and passionately. Iced tea can be found, but it is not widely popular.

TEA (MEAL)

An early supper, sometimes for children. Usually served around four or five p.m.

161

TEACAKE

This may look obvious, but the term can mean different things, depending on where you are. In most of the UK, a teacake is a sweet, yeast-based bread bun containing mixed dried fruit. It's usually served toasted and spread with butter. In many parts of northern England, however, "teacake" is used to describe a large bread roll. In Scotland, it can refer to a Tunnock's Teacake, a chocolate-covered marshmallow on a cookie. Oh, and there's also the "tea cake," which is actually a cake in the traditional sense. No one said this was going to be easy!

> "American-style iced tea is the perfect drink for a hot, sunny day. It's never really caught on in the UK, probably because the last time we had a hot, sunny day was back in 1957."
>
> —Tom Holt

TIN

A can of something, e.g., a "tin of peas."

TOAD IN THE HOLE

A traditional dish of sausage baked in a Yorkshire pudding batter. No one believes the dish has ever been made with real toads, and the origin of this term remains murky.

TREACLE

Molasses.

TRIFLE

A beautiful and delicious layered dessert consisting of fruit, sponge cake soaked in fortified wine, and custard, and usually topped with whipped cream. Made in a glass bowl, so the layers are visible from the side. See **Custard** page 139.

TROLLEY

A grocery cart or luggage cart.

TUCK

Slang for food that children eat as a snack at school.

WELSH RAREBIT

Savory cheese sauce poured over toasted bread. The traditional version of the sauce recipe calls for grated cheese mixed with egg, beer or milk, Worcestershire sauce, mustard, and cayenne pepper. A favorite of everyone from college students to diners in fine restaurants. Sometimes pronounced—and even spelled—"rabbit," but there's no rabbit in it!

> "There are hardly two things more peculiarly English than Welsh rarebit and Irish Stew."
> —G.K. Chesterton

WHITE COFFEE

Coffee with milk. You might get a puzzled look if you ask for cream in your coffee.

YORKSHIRE PUDDING

A batter of flour, milk, and eggs placed in a hot oven until it puffs up. It was traditionally made in a large, flat rectangular tray and served ahead of the main course to fill people up. Today, it's made in individual portions and often served as a Sunday roast side dish. See **Sunday roast** page 160.

9.

Geography and the Countryside

THE AMERICAN CONCEPT OF REGIONAL DIFFERENCES, ACCENTS, and cultural values is applicable in the UK, but on a much smaller and compact scale. English people who vacation in the USA frequently comment, "It's just so big there, the houses, the grocery stores, the cars, and blimey! Those huge food portions!"

The UK is roughly the size of Michigan (both are just under one hundred thousand square miles). Of course, it also has a longer coastline and a much longer history, both of which have influenced British culture. I must emphasize that London, although the UK's largest city, is not representative of the whole country. In fact, resentment simmers against London's inequitable influence among all who live elsewhere.

In the UK, every geographic area considers itself to be unique and special. Each region has features, customs, colloquialisms, and practices the locals defend vigorously. These carefully guarded cultural icons include everything from recipes for Yorkshire pudding and words for bread to the characteristics of a perfect "cuppa."

Because regionalism is delightfully alive and well in the UK, it's a wonderful place to be a tourist. Traveling from coast to coast means something completely different from what it means in the USA. In the UK, a cross-country trip can take as little as a day, but such a journey still offers a wealth of charming local diversity.

ALLOTMENT

A small portion of land, usually owned by the local town council, that is rented for a small amount for the purpose of growing vegetables and flowers and also to provide green space to urbanites. An allotment usually has a storage structure that often serves as a "man cave" or a "she shed." An entire quirky culture of tea, greenhouses, and growing advice has grown up around allotments since World War II, when they were a primary source of food. Several years after moving to the UK, I was eager to experience something truly English. I applied for, and was granted, an allotment I still have and enjoy.

AONB

An abbreviation for "Area of Outstanding Natural Beauty." Often seen on maps, it is an official government designation that strictly limits development. Examples include the coastline of the Gower Peninsula in Wales and the Chiltern Hills in Buckinghamshire. While the term "AONB" is used in England, Wales, and Northern Ireland, Scotland calls these "National Scenic Areas," or "NSAs" for short.

BEN NEVIS

The UK's tallest mountain at 1,345 meters/4,400 feet. It's possible to hike to the top of Ben Nevis, which is located near Fort William in Scotland. Many years ago, my daughter and I took this hike, but then we were useless for anything the whole next day. It is a long and arduous trip, and proper footwear is a must. Even so, more than one hundred thousand people do this every summer. Don't try it in the winter months—winter storms and deep snow make it dangerous. There's a large cairn at the summit, along with a ruined observatory with fantastic 360-degree vistas. It's always windy at the top, and there are no services en route, so take water. Even if you don't climb the mountain, the train ride from Glasgow to Fort William is terrific in its own right.

BLACK COUNTRY

The heavily industrial area in the West Midlands of England west of Birmingham, including most of the four Metropolitan District Council areas of Dudley, Sandwell, Walsall, and Wolverhampton. It's said that the Black Country gained its name in the mid-nineteenth century from the smoke produced by the many thousands of ironworking foundries and forges in the area.

BLIGHTY

Slang for Britain. The word is also military slang for "a wound."

BOIS

A French word for wood or tree, sometimes used in place names in the UK. A couple of well-known examples are Theydon Bois (pronounced "Boyz") in Essex and Chesham Bois in Buckinghamshire.

BOW BELLS

The bells of St Mary-le-Bow in Cheapside, London. Tradition holds that to be a true Cockney, you must have been born within earshot of these bells.

BRECON BEACONS

A national park in mid-Wales near the town of Brecon, that encompasses a range of sandstone peaks and two mountain ranges called the Black Mountains. The park contains some of the most distinctive and spectacular valleys, waterfalls, caves, and peaks in the UK.

BRIDLEWAY

A footpath for walking, horseback riding, and bicycling. Horse-drawn vehicles are not allowed. Cyclists must yield to pedestrians and horseback riders.

BRITAIN

A contraction for "Great Britain," which is the union of England, Scotland, and Wales. Northern Ireland is not part of Britain, but it is part of the United Kingdom of Great Britain and Northern Ireland. People usually self-identify as being from one of these countries.

BROADS

The Norfolk Broads, a low-lying region of eastern England in Norfolk and Suffolk with wide, shallow lakes connected by rivers and small streams. The Broads are a wildlife and recreational preserve.

BROWN SPACE

An abandoned industrial site.

CANAL

A constructed waterway dug during the Industrial Revolution for transporting raw materials and finished goods. Canals fell into disuse and disrepair in the mid-twentieth century but are now used for boating and recreation.

"If countries were named after the words you first hear when you go there, England would have to be called 'Damn It.'"
—Georg Christoph Lichtenberg, *Aphorisms*

CHANNEL ISLANDS

The group of islands that lie eighty miles off the southern coast of England, closer to the coast of Normandy than to the UK. Consisting of Guernsey, Jersey, Alderney, Herne, and Sark, they have a combined population of about two hundred thousand people. Known as British Crown Dependencies, they're independent from the UK, but the residents are British citizens.

COPSE

A thicket or grove of trees growing very close to each other, usually all the same species. (Pronounced "cops.")

CORNWALL

A county in the southern and westernmost part of England, known for its wild and rugged coastline. Historically, the area was known for fishing and tin mining, but today it's a tourist mecca. Popular attractions include the Eden Project, Helston, the Lizard peninsula, Land's End, St Ives, and Tintagel Castle. Cornwall has more sunny days than any other mainland UK county.

DALE

An open valley. The term is used primarily in Scotland and northern England. Dales are surrounded by steep hills called "fells." See **Fell** page 172.

> "The biggest difference between England and America is that England has history, while America has geography."
> —Neil Gaiman

DOMESDAY TOWNS

Settlements first recorded in 1086 in the Domesday Book, a census commissioned by William the Conqueror.

DOWNS

An archaic term for ancient and rounded grass-covered hills that form a distinct and large geographical feature on the landscape. They're characterized by the lack of trees and used mainly as pasture. The name comes from "dun," the Old English word for hill. Downs are sometimes also called "wolds," as in the Cotswolds.

> "The English winter is long, cold and wet, just like the English summer."
> —Benny Bellamacina, *Philosophical Uplifting Quotes and Poems*

EAST MIDLANDS

The eastern part of the Midlands, a region of central England. Its main cities are Nottingham, Leicester, Lincoln Derby, and Northampton. Lincoln Cathedral and Sherwood Forest are two of the area's best-known destinations.

EAST ANGLIA

A region that includes the counties of Norfolk and Suffolk and parts of Cambridgeshire, known for flat landscapes and wide-open vistas. Generically and non-specifically, the area is sometimes also referred to as the "East of England." The central town of the region is Norwich. See **Norfolk** page 179.

FELL

A small, unforested mountain or large hill, common in the Lake District in Cumbria. Popular with hikers known as "fell walkers."

FENS

The Fens, also called Fenland, are a natural region of reclaimed marshland in eastern England between Lincoln and Cambridge.

FOOTPATH

A general term for any pedestrian pathway. It can be applied to a sidewalk but is more generally used to describe a path not associated with a road. See **Public footpath** page 181.

FORTH BRIDGE

The rail bridge across the Firth of Forth in Scotland. Known around the world for its distinctive red steel cantilever design. Opened in 1890, the structure has been designated a UNESCO World Heritage Site. It is sometimes called the Forth Rail Bridge to distinguish it from the nearby highway bridge, although that has never been its official name. The only way to cross the bridge is on a train traveling between Edinburgh and Aberdeen.

I have traveled around most of the world, and in the springtime there's nowhere I'd rather be than in the English countryside. I've often wondered whether it's because everything seems so alive and intense. The daffodils seem yellower, the sun seems brighter, the dogs seem doggier, and the green is the most intense and verdant green I've ever seen. Or, alternatively, is it because the previous twelve weeks were so wet, gray, and miserable that it just seems that way?

Generally, the skies cloud over, and the rains start in mid-November. Activities move indoors, and by January the rain has usually changed to snow. By the end of March, everyone's so tired of having wet feet and sniffles that they just can't wait for spring!

—M.H.

GOWER PENINSULA

Also known as "The Gower," this peninsula in South Wales juts out westward into the Bristol Channel. At its tip is a rock formation with a roaring blow hole known as the Worm's Head. It's a fantastic adventure to walk the coastal path to visit "the Worm" and nearby sea caves, but be careful of the local tides.

I was staying with friends in Llanmadoc on the Gower peninsula when I decided to spend the day walking along the Gower's north coast. It's a great coastline to explore, and I particularly wanted to see the abandoned Victorian lighthouse at Whiteford Point. More than seven hours of happy experience later, I took a late afternoon shortcut across an empty and dry bay toward home. I knew about the treacherous tides in the area and had been warned several times, "You can't outrun them." I hadn't calculated the time accurately. About halfway across, I could see the tide approaching fast. I realized that whether I turned back or ran forward, I wasn't going to make it to either side in time. My only option was to make a sharp right-angle turn and run as fast as I could toward the nearest shore, a distance of about four hundred yards. Running at full tilt, I soon felt water beneath my feet and remembered those dire words about outrunning the tide. By the time I reached the cliff face, I was knee deep in the surging sea and had no choice but to start climbing vertically, clinging to clumps of grass and protruding bits of rock. I finally reached a level above the tideline and hung on until I caught my breath and collected my wits—at least half an hour. Cautiously, and ever so slowly, I grasped grass and rock to inch upward until I could feel the vertical slowly becoming more horizontal. At the top, I was greeting by several curious sheep who seemed to be casting a critical eye on this stupid human creature.

Later that evening in the pub, I told my friends the story. They were upset. They claimed that if I had drowned out there, it would have ruined this holiday spot for them.

—M.H.

GREENBELT

An area of land around a town or city that, by law, cannot be developed. Existing houses within a greenbelt area are allowed to remain, but no new construction is permitted.

> "Oh, to be in England now that April's there ..."
> —Robert Browning

HEADLAND

Palisades that jut out from the coast into the sea. Along England's south coast, the headlands are tall chalk cliffs that form the "White Cliffs of Dover."

HECTARE

A unit of surface area. A hectare equals about two and a half acres.

HEDGE LAYING

The ancient practice of creating a hedge by "pleaching," or partially cutting the stems of the hedging plants and interweaving them. This produces an extremely thick and strong hedge. Also known as hedge weaving.

HIGHLANDS AND ISLANDS

The area of northwest Scotland that includes the Highlands
and the isles of Orkney, Shetland, Ust, and Stornaway. The
Highlands boast some of the world's most stunning scenery
and have been featured in several James Bond films and
Alfred Hitchcock's *The 39 Steps*.

HIGH STREET

The main business street of a town. "You'll be able to find
that down the high street."

ISLES OF SCILLY

This archipelago of ten small islands (only five are inhabited)
forms a UK county and lies just off the westernmost point
of Cornwall. St Marys is the largest island, followed by
Tresco and St Martins. The influence of the Gulf Stream
makes Scilly warmer than the rest of the UK and a popular
holiday destination.

ISLE OF MAN

A large self-governing island in the Irish Sea, officially
listed as a "Crown Dependency." It is about ten miles wide
and thirty miles long with a central mountain range and
rocky coastline. The island is known for the indigenous
Manx cat, a unique ginger-colored feline that has no tail.

ISLE OF WIGHT

Located five miles off the south UK coast opposite
Portsmouth and Southampton, this 150-square-mile island

is the largest coastal island. The island is known for the Isle of Wight Festival and the Cowes Powerboat Races. The "Needles" lighthouse on the far western tip of the island offers stunning views out into the English Channel.

JURASSIC COAST

This UNESCO World Heritage Site on the south coast of England stretches from Exmouth to Bournemouth. 185 million years of geological history from the Mesozoic Era are visible here. Fossils of ammonites and marine life are abundant. Lulworth Cove has always been my favorite starting spot for exploring the area along the South West Coastal Path.

LAKE DISTRICT

A national park in Cumbria that includes Lake Windermere—England's largest—and Scafell Pike, its tallest mountain. It was designated a UNESCO World Heritage Site in 2017.

LAND'S END

The most westerly point of mainland Britain, located eight miles west of Penzance. While the coastline is owned by the National Trust and remains undeveloped, the adjacent land is owned by a private company that has built tourist attractions that are a blight on the beautiful landscape. You can get to the coast without paying a fee, but it's worth paying for parking to avoid a long walk. See **South West** page 183.

LLANFAIRPWLLGWYNGYLLGOGERYCHWYRNDROBWLLLLANTYSILIOGOGOGOCH

Commonly shortened to "Llanfair PG," this is a town on the island of Anglesey in Wales. It's the longest place name in Europe.

LOCH LOMOND & THE TROSSACHS

One of two national parks in Scotland, the other one being the Cairngorms.

LONDINIUM

The settlement established by the Romans on the banks of the Thames that eventually grew into the modern city of London.

LOOKOUT

A high spot overlooking a large expanse. Wendover Lookout is an example. Such sites were important for early settlements as lookouts for approaching danger.

> "Wensleydale lies between Tuesleydale and Thursleydale!"
> —Arthur Smith

MIDLANDS

The industrialized central part of England including Warwickshire, Northamptonshire, Leicestershire, Nottinghamshire, Derbyshire, and Staffordshire. Often unofficially divided into the East Midlands with Nottingham at its center, and the West Midlands with Birmingham in the center.

MOOR

A large area of open high grassland, usually with acidic soil and poor drainage. The UK has several famous moors, including:

- Exmoor—Devon and Somerset
- Bodmin—Cornwall
- North Yorkshire Moors—Yorkshire
- Dartmoor National Park—Devon

Dartmoor was the setting of Sir Arthur Conan Doyle's *The Hound of the Baskervilles*. Hiking and walking in the 860,000 acres of the UK's moors is a popular activity with American tourists.

NEW TOWN

A town, or part of a town, that has been developed separate from the original "old town" but keeps the same name. Examples include Amersham New Town and Basildon New Town. The old and the new may have some degree of integration with one another, sharing shops, facilities, and street layout. See **Old town** page 180.

NORFOLK

A popular tourist destination, Norfolk is a large county seventy-five miles north of London bordered by Suffolk, Cambridgeshire, and Lincolnshire. It is a low-lying area encompassing The Broads National Park and internationally important wildlife preserves. Norwich serves as the administrative center of the area and is the most complete medieval city in the UK. See **Broads** page 169.

NORTHERN IRELAND

One of the countries making up the United Kingdom, not to be confused with the separate and independent Republic of Ireland. The capital city of Belfast is home to the Titanic Museum. The Mountains of Mourne are likely to be the location of Northern Ireland's first national park. Its north coast features the Giant's Causeway, an amazing rock formation made up of more than forty thousand interlocking basalt columns. Other attractions in Northern Ireland include:
- Peace Bridge, Derry/Londonderry
- Derry City Walls
- The Ulster Transport and Folk Museum
- The Carrick-a-Rede Rope Bridge
- The Old Bushmills Distillery, the oldest working distillery in Ireland
- The Dark Hedges, Ballymoney. This row of beech trees was recently featured as The King's Road in HBO's *Game of Thrones*.

OLD TOWN

The original part of a town that has developed a somewhat separate New Town with the same name. Examples include Amersham Old Town and Milton Keynes Old Town. The old and the new may have some degree of integration with one another, sharing shops, facilities, and street layout. This evolution happens for a variety of reasons, including historic preservation, expanding population, housing needs, access to rail services, or environmental considerations.

ORDNANCE SURVEY MAPS

Wonderfully detailed maps of specific sections of the English countryside. Available in different scales, they're used a lot by walking and hiking enthusiasts. First developed in the mid-1700s for the military, they're now produced by a government-owned company today. Maps for all of Britain are available, both in print and online.

PUBLIC FOOTPATH

A pathway through private land that's open to the public. This is a very old tradition in England and can be the source of controversy.

ROMAN BRITAIN

The Romans first invaded Britain in 55 BC and occupied the country for about four centuries. Roman influence can still be found all over Britain in the form of place names and archaeological remains, including buildings, roads, and walls. The largest of these is Hadrian's Wall, which ran for seventy-three miles across the neck of northern England. It's still walkable in many places and is ranked, even in ruined form, as the world's largest Roman artifact.

-SHIRE

A suffix attached to a county name, as in Leicestershire, Yorkshire, and Buckinghamshire. It originally referred to an area of rural countryside with an agricultural lifestyle. Romanticized and made famous by English artists such as Constable and authors such as J.R.R. Tolkien. ("Shire" rhymes with "hire" when it stands alone. As a suffix, it is pronounced "-sher.")

SHIRES

"The shires" is a general term meaning "out in the country."

SLAG HEAP

Tailings from coal mines and waste from iron and steel manufacturing. These often large and potentially dangerous black hills were once a common sight across parts of the UK, but many have now been landscaped to create parks and nature preserves.

SNOWDONIA

The Area of Outstanding Natural Beauty surrounding Mt Snowdon in northwestern Wales. See **AONB** page 166.

SOUTH DOWNS

The South Downs are an area of chalk hills running sixty-eight miles west to east across southern England and easily accessible from London. The area is a popular destination for walkers, mountain bikers, and horseback riders.

SOUTH WEST

The south western peninsula of England jutting westward into the Atlantic, one of the UK's favorite holiday destinations. The South West encompasses the counties of Dorset, Devon, and Cornwall, Dartmoor and Exmoor National Parks, and the cities of Bath, Plymouth, and Bristol. See **Land's End** page 177.

THAMES ESTUARY

The eastern most point of the River Thames, where it flows into the North Sea. Partially saline and affected by tides, it serves as a wildlife habitat in the counties of Essex and Kent.

THAMES (RIVER)

Pronounced "Tems," this is the river running west to east through London. Mispronounce it if you want to be instantly identified as a tourist.

TOR

A large exposed rocky pinnacle at the top of a hill.

VALE

A valley. This term is used frequently in place names. One example is the Vale of Glanmorgan in southern Wales.

VALLEYS

"The Valleys" is a partially urbanized area of South Wales that contains two valleys that run parallel to each other north to south. They cover the area from Carmarthenshire in the East to Monmouthshire in the West.

WASH

"The Wash" is a shallow inlet of the North Sea on the east coast of England, between Lincolnshire and Norfolk.

WEST COUNTRY

The western counties of England. For those living in London, the West Country begins in Reading.

WEST MIDLANDS

"The West Midlands" is a metropolitan county of central England that includes the cities of Birmingham, Coventry, and Wolverhampton.

YEW

An ancient species of evergreen tree traditionally grown on the grounds of a church.

YORKSHIRE

Nicknamed "God's Own County," probably by Yorkshire residents, it's England's largest county. It lies to the north-west of London and encompasses the cities of York, Leeds, Sheffield, and Bradford. It's also known for its moors and national parks.

10.

Around the Home

ONE INESCAPABLE DIFFERENCE IN THE VALUE SYSTEMS OF Americans and the British is their sense of space. As an American, I grew up with the feeling that there was always more space, so we could have a large house and a large yard without too much consideration of one day running out of countryside. The cars were large, the buildings were larger, and the country was enormous. As populations increased, cities just appropriated additional countryside, and life went on. The same cannot be said of the British psyche.

Space has always been a limited and precious commodity in the UK, and people born here grow up with a sense that it needs to be used sparingly. As a result, one of the first impressions Americans have is that everything is smaller. The cars are small, the houses are small, and there isn't enough space to have dedicated rooms for every function. For example, the washing machine is often tucked under a counter in the kitchen rather than placed in a separate laundry room. In recent years, larger American-style appliances have become more popular in the UK.

Housing is much more tightly compacted in the UK, because the population density—over seven hundred people per square mile—is nearly eight times that of the US—fewer than one hundred people per square mile. Having too few homes for too many people has caused a steep and inexorable rise in housing prices. Whether a rent or loan payment, these represent a significantly larger percentage of income in the UK than in the USA. In London, for example, residents pay as much as half their gross income on housing.

Many American visitors to the UK stay in hotels. Accommodations can be quite nice, but rooms are often smaller than those in equivalent American establishments. With the rise of rentals by owners, more Americans have the opportunity to stay in a British home. This section should help clear up any mysteries about domestic terminology.

BASIN

>   A sink. In London and surrounding areas, this would be pronounced "bi-son," resulting in the old joke, "What's the difference between a buffalo and a bison? You can't wash your hands in a buffalo."

BATH

>   A bathtub.

BATHROOM

>   The room where the bathtub is located. If you ask for the bathroom, Brits will think you want a bath. If you'd like

to use the toilet, then ask for the loo or the toilet. See **Loo** page 193.

BBC

The British Broadcasting Corporation. Formed in 1926, it is a publicly owned corporation supported by the TV license fee. Also known in slang terms as "The Beeb" and "Auntie" because of its historically conservative views on morality and social issues. See **TV license fee** page 200.

BEDSIDE TABLE

A nightstand or small table placed next to the head of the bed. It may contain drawers or not.

BIN

A trash can. It could be a small one used inside the house or a big one used outside. See **Dustbin** page 190.

BITS AND BOBS

An assortment of small things not related to one another, e.g., pens, spare keys, or a small jar containing assorted screws, paper clips, and anything else that "might be useful someday." "This the drawer where I keep all my bits and bobs."

BLOWER

Slang for an analog landline telephone. "I'm speaking to Dad on the blower tonight." Said to originate from the old communication tubes used to link upstairs and downstairs in the homes of the wealthy. Blowing down the tube would sound a whistle at the other end, alerting a servant. Also known as a "trombone."

BOG

A toilet. Like Americans who insist on calling a toilet a "bathroom" or a "rest room," the British have a plethora of euphemisms for the toilet, including:
- Loo
- Khazi (karzy)
- Privy
- WC (water closet)
- Lavatory
- Comfort room
- Netty
- Potty (used only by little children)
- Small room

See **Loo** page 193, **Bathroom** page 186, and **WC** page 200.

BOG STANDARD

Run of the mill, nothing extraordinary, without accessories.

BOILER

The gas central heating unit in a house that also provides hot water.

CHRISTMAS CRACKER

A decorated cardboard tube wrapped in colorful paper that emits a large "BANG!" when it is pulled apart by two Christmas dinner guests. Inside are small trinket gifts, a written joke, and a paper hat or crown that is then worn at the dinner table. Crackers are famous for their very bad jokes.

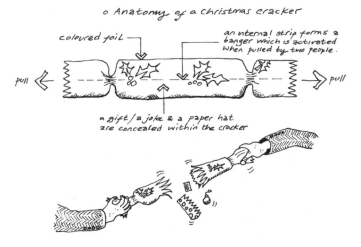

o Anatomy of a christmas cracker

coloured foil

an internal strip forms a banger which is activated when pulled by two people.

pull   pull

a gift / a joke & a paper hat are concealed within the cracker

Why did the sausage roll?
Because it saw the apple turnover!
—A standard Christmas cracker joke

CHUCK OUT

To throw something out.

CLING FILM

Plastic wrap. Thin, transparent polyethylene used for wrapping food. "Saran Wrap" is an American trademark.

COME ROUND

To visit someone's house. To wake up or become aware.

CONSUMER UNIT

The circuit breaker box of a house.

COOKER

A kitchen cooking range or stove. See **Hob** page 192.

COT

A baby crib.

DUSTBIN

A garbage can. A large container outside your house, used for holding waste until it is taken away by the garbage man.

DUVET

A bed-size comforter traditionally filled with feathers or down and used as a blanket. The duvet is usually placed inside a washable cover and used with or without a top sheet. (Pronounced "DOO-vay.")

EIDERDOWN

A quilt. The name comes from the feathers of the seagoing eider duck that were used to stuff the quilt or duvet.

FACE CLOTH

A washcloth.

FAIRY LIQUID

A brand name of a popular dishwashing liquid.

FILOFAX

A brand name for a type of day planner or organizer popular in the 1990s. Once a status symbol and still in use, it is similar in size and structure to Franklin Covey binders in the USA. Filofax inserts and Franklin inserts are interchangeable.

FIRST FLOOR

The second floor.

FLANNEL

A washcloth.

FLEX

An extension cord used for household appliances.

GARDEN

A yard. A house's outdoor leisure area.

GROUND FLOOR

The first floor (or ground floor). In the UK, "first floor" means the level above ground floor, which is called the "second floor" in the USA.

GLADSTONE BAG

A piece of hand luggage traditionally having a hinged frame. Named for British prime minister William E. Gladstone.

GOGGLEBOX (GOGGLE-BOX)

Slang for a television set.

GUY FAWKES NIGHT

November 5 is when many people have parties, fireworks, and bonfires on which they burn an effigy of "the Guy." It began as a way of remembering the attempt by Guy Fawkes and his followers to blow up the Houses of Parliament in 1605. Guy Fawkes Night is often referred to as "Bonfire Night." Guy Fawkes Night is not a legal holiday.

HAIR GRIP

A bobby pin.

HIRE PURCHASE

An installment plan, commonly abbreviated HP. Also known in slang as "the drip." See **The never-never** page 36.

HOB

A cooktop or hotplate.

HOOVER

A vacuum cleaner. Also a verb meaning "to vacuum." The original building that housed the Hoover headquarters in

Perivale has been remodeled into apartments and is famous for its art deco architecture.

IMMERSION HEATER

Electric heating elements often found in boilers as a back-up to the main water heating system.

IVORIES

Piano keys. Can also mean dice or a person's teeth.

KETTLE

An electric appliance for boiling water very quickly. Ubiquitous in kitchens in the UK and essential for the English cup of tea.

LARDER

A pantry. Historically, it was a room in a British home dedicated to storing food. Many were equipped with cool storage areas to place food before serving or to keep leftovers. Some had marble shelves for storing meat.

LEVER ARCH FILE

A three-ring binder.

LODGER

A person renting a room in a house.

LOO

A toilet. See **Bog** page 188 and **WC** page 200.

LOO ROLL OR BOG ROLL
Toilet paper.

LOUNGE
A living room.

MADE-TO-MEASURE
Referring to an item or items that are custom fabricated to specific measurements. Examples include made-to-measure drapes and made-to-measure suits—as opposed to "off-the-rack."

MEDIUM WAVE
A range of electromagnetic waves between 300 KHz and 3 MHz used for broadcast radio. The broadcast spectrum is divided differently in the UK. In addition to AM and FM, there is Medium wave.

METHYLATED SPIRITS
Denatured alcohol. Ethanol that has been made unfit for drinking by the addition of methanol, pyridine and purple coloring.

MID-TERRACE HOUSE
A house, often a "two up-two down," that has similar houses attached to both sides. See **Terraced house** page 21 and **Two up-two down** page 22.

> "In this country, people are sitting on chairs in their houses
> that Americans would have behind glass in a museum!"
> —Max Fisher

MIXER TAP

A faucet that mixes the hot- and cold-water lines. These seem to have arrived late to the UK and, although now more common, are still not found everywhere. In the USA, these are commonly known as "mixer valves" and are the predominant kind of faucets.

NET CURTAINS

Sheer curtains under the drapes. They are also used to describe a nosey person, e.g., "She spends all day peeping from behind her net curtains."

NOUGHTS AND CROSSES

Tic-tac-toe.

OFF-PUTTING

Referring to an event or incident that has made someone or something no longer attractive or desirable. "That's really off-putting" and "That's put me right off."

OLD MONEY

Refers to the UK currency before 1971, when the system was decimalized. See **Bob** page 57, **Florin** page 309 and **Shilling** page 312.

OXFAM

An international organization established in England in 1942 to provide famine relief, training, and financial aid to people in developing countries and disaster areas.

PARAFFIN

Kerosene often used in old lamps and heaters.

PELMET

A valence, or a decorative box-like structure at the top of a window that conceals the tops of the curtains and the rod they hang from. In the UK, a valence is found on a bed and used to hide the mattress.

PLAIT

Braided hair.

PLASTER

A Band-Aid. In the UK, the brand Elastoplast has become a generic name for this, sometimes called a "sticking plaster." This term can also mean a plaster cast, but those are more commonly referred to as "pots."

PLUG HOLE

A hole at the lowest point of a bath, basin or sink, known as the "drain," which can be stopped with a plug.

PONG

A really bad smell.

POOH BEAR
> Winnie-the-Pooh, the bear friend of Christopher Robin in the children's books written by A.A. Milne.

POST CODE
> The suffix attached to all addresses, usually including letters as well as numbers. Similar to the American zip code.

POUFFE
> An upholstered foot stool. (Pronounced "poof.")

POWER POINT
> An electrical outlet. Also commonly referred to as a "socket." ("There are never enough sockets in this house!") Not the Microsoft program!

PRAM
> A "perambulator" or baby carriage that has four wheels. The infant lies flat.

PRIVET
> A species of dense shrub commonly used for hedges because it can be trimmed neatly.

PRIVY
> A toilet, usually referring to a freestanding outhouse.

PUSHCHAIR
> A stroller.

RELATE

The government-supported marriage/relationship counselling service.

RSPCA

An animal-protection charity founded in 1824. RSPCA
stands for the Royal Society for the Prevention of Cruelty
to Animals.

SAMARITANS

An organization of volunteers who offer telephone support
and counselling to people in despair and at risk for suicide.

SERVIETTE

Napkin.

SETTEE

A sofa or couch.

SHEARS

Large scissors used in tailoring and gardening.

SITTING ROOM

The room in an English home, usually the room nearest
the front door, where guests sit. Americans would call it
the "living room." See **Two-up, two-down** page 22 and
Lounge page 194.

SKIP

A dumpster.

SMALL ROOM

A room containing a toilet fixture. See **Bog** page 188,
Loo page 193, and **WC** page 200.

STONE

A measurement of weight equaling 14 pounds. Talk to a
Brit about someone who weighs 250 pounds, and it won't
mean much. It's 17 stone, 12 pounds in the UK.

TAP

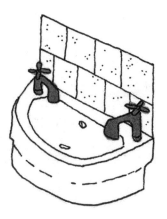

Faucet. Britain still has a lot
of housing that does not provide
the pleasures of a mixer tap.
I'm uncertain why this is but
even in some high-end hotels
you'll either freeze or scald
yourself with separate cold and
hot sink faucets.

TROMBONE

See **Blower** page 187.

TURN DOWN THE BED

To pull back the blankets, covers, and top sheet halfway
in preparation for bedtime. Although most people in the

UK now use duvets, the term is still used in hotels and on cruise ships, which tout their "turn-down service."

TV LICENSE (LICENCE)

Yes, believe it or not, all televisions in the UK require a license to operate. The fee goes indirectly to the BBC to assist in new productions. In the current political climate, this fee may be on its way out.

WC

The toilet. This is an abbreviation for "Water closet." See **Loo** page 193, **Bog** page 188, and **Small room** page 199.

WASHING UP

The act of washing dirty dishes after a meal.

WATER BUTT

A barrel that collects rainwater for use in the garden.

11.

People, Professions, and Businesses

"IT'S THE PEOPLE THAT MAKE THE PLACE!" WE'VE ALL HEARD this before, and nowhere is it truer than in the UK. They're a fascinating study in human differences. I've often thought that just when I think I've got it figured out, one hundred miles up the road and you've got to start all over again. Two overwhelming influences on this phenomenon are the historic regionalism of the country and the diverse cultures reflected in its population.

Regions in the UK have always had distinct cultural values, traditions, language, accents, and allegiances. Although modern life has reduced the intensity of these differences, it has not eliminated them. They provide delightful motivation for American visitors to explore more than just London. When I first arrived in the UK, I was amazed at the ability of older people to tell what city a person came from just by their accent. Some even claimed they could identify the street a person lived on by their accent.

London is one of the most ethnically diverse cities in the world. This amazing diversity means that over 250 languages, cultures, cuisines, and religions form the city's cultural landscape. But this

201

is nothing new—in ancient times, the UK was a Roman territory for nearly four hundred years. That period brought a great influx of people and goods from all across the Roman Empire. Recent skeletal discoveries made while excavating for railroad construction have revealed that Londinium contained a multitude of Mediterranean and North African cultures. Today, all the cities of the UK are home to people from around the globe.

ARGIE
> Slang for an Argentinean.

ASIAN
> In the UK, this term is generally used to describe people from the Indian Subcontinent, including India, Pakistan, Bangladesh, and Sri Lanka. These countries are also commonly referred to as "South Asia." (To Americans, Canadians, Australians, and New Zealanders, "Asian" means belonging to or relating to China, Japan, or countries near them, so take note of this different usage.)

> "Nothing gives the English more pleasure, in a quiet but determined sort of way, than to do things oddly."
> —Bill Bryson, *Notes from a Small Island*

AUSSIE
> An Australian.

BARRISTER

A lawyer who represents clients in court. This role differs from that of a solicitor, whose job it is to provide legal advice and prepare cases for court. In the movies, barristers are like trial lawyers in the Unites States, and solicitors are the attorneys who do all the work outside of a courtroom. See **Solicitor** page 214.

BARMY ARMY

A wild or enthusiastic group of people—particularly the rabid fans of the English national cricket team and Wimbledon tennis.

BELT AND BRACES MAN

Slang for an overly cautious person. Same as "belt and suspenders" in the USA.

BLOKE

A man, guy, "some guy." What guys call other guys.

BOBBY

A policeman. "Bobby" is a less frequently used term these days other than in the context of "You never see bobbies on the street these days" or the pre-election promise of politicians to "put more bobbies on the street." The word comes from the name of Sir Robert Peel, who founded London's Metropolitan Police force in 1829.

BOOKIE

A bookmaker. There are bookies on every high street (main street) in the UK. As well as offering odds on horse racing, football (soccer), tennis, golf, rugby, any other sport, and political events, they accept bets on the weather—like whether snow will fall on Christmas Day. They also have slot machines.

BRUMMIE

A person who comes from the Birmingham area in central England. Also an English dialect that is spoken in the West Midlands.

BUILDERS' MERCHANT

The business where a builder obtains materials, including wood, masonry, tools, and roofing. It usually sells retail as well as wholesale. Most similar to Home Depot or Lowes in the USA.

BUILDING SOCIETY

An organization set up to help members buy their own homes. In the past, their services were limited to savings and loans or mortgages. Most of the larger ones are now virtually indistinguishable from banks in terms of the services they offer. The remaining difference is that building society profits are distributed to members rather than to shareholders. Similar to an American credit union.

CHARITY SHOP

A shop that receives donations of clothing, kitchenware, and household goods, which are then sold to support the sponsoring charity. This type of fundraising is widely used by the UK's large hospice movement and also by national charities of all kinds.

CHELSEA PENSIONERS

Veterans of the British Army who have surrendered their Army Pension in exchange for admission as permanent residents of the Royal Hospital Chelsea (founded in 1692 by King Charles II). They are often seen in their bright red uniforms representing the military services in parades.

CHEMIST

This can be either the drug store, the business, or the pharmacist who works there. "I need to stop at the chemist's while we're out."

CHUM

A mate, friend, buddy.

CITIZENS ADVICE

A network of more than three hundred independent charities that provide free, confidential advice on everything from social benefits, debt, and health to housing, immigration, and consumer issues. Services are provided by both professional staff and volunteers via website and telephone as well as in person at its many locations.

COCKNEY

Technically speaking, a Cockney is someone who was born in the East End of London, traditionally within earshot of Bow Bells, but the term has broadened to encompass virtually anyone with a working-class London accent.

COLLIERY

A coal mine. Those working in and around a colliery are more likely to use the term "pit." Given the historical significance of coal to the UK, abandoned collieries are a common sight all over the country.

COMMONER

From a royal point of view, a commoner is anyone not of any royal, noble, or aristocratic lineage. May a royal marry a commoner? Well, Prince Charles did when he married Camilla, and both of his sons have, too.

COPPER

A once-derogatory but now commonplace term for a policeman, derived from the word "cop," meaning to take or to seize, e.g., "Cop a look at this!" This evolved into copper (one who seizes) to describe the police in the mid-nineteenth century. It may also refer to a penny, e.g., "I've only got coppers in my pocket." Or "Look, he's coppering up; he must be completely skint." (Skint = broke.)

CRUMPET

Slang for a woman. It's increasingly used to refer to either gender, meaning "an object of sexual desire."

DAD'S ARMY

This was Second World War slang for the Home Guard. It is also a nickname for any political organization, sports team, or other group whose members are thought to be inept or too old to be effective.

DICK WHITTINGTON

The Lord Mayor of London three times in the fifteenth century. Most British people know the stories about him: that he was running away from London with his cat when he was a boy, but thought he heard the Bow church bells telling him to "Turn again, Whittington, thrice Lord Mayor of London," and that he became rich by selling his cat to a foreign king. See **Bow Bells** page 168.

DUSTMAN

An old term for a garbage collector. Household refuse once consisted largely of ashes—or dust—from domestic fires. The name of this job evolved to "binman," and the task is now carried out by a "refuse collector."

FARE-DODGER

Someone who rides public transportation without paying the fare.

FISHMONGER

A person who sells fish.

GEEZER

Usually a complimentary term for a dude. "He knows what's what—he's a real geezer." Or, even better, "He's a diamond geezer." On the other hand, a used car salesman might well be described as "a dodgy geezer."

GEORDIE

Someone from Newcastle upon Tyne.

GIRL GUIDE

A Girl Scout.

GLASWEGIAN

A person from Glasgow. Also sometimes referred to as "Weegies."

GREAT UNWASHED

"The great unwashed" is a disparaging term for ordinary people, coined by the Victorian novelist and playwright Edward Bulwer-Lytton.

GREENGROCER

A seller of fruits and vegetables. Traditionally, many foods in the UK were sold in specialty shops, including bakeries, butcher shops, and greengrocers.

GUVNOR, GUV

A contraction of "governor" used as a term of respect for someone in a position of power, authority, or seniority, or simply "boss." It is frequently shortened to "guv" in face-to-face communication, e.g., "How can I help you, guv?"

> Each day while walking to the university, I would pass people on Marylebone High Street asking for money. Many were obviously homeless, and without exception they addressed me as "guvnor." Not understanding what this meant, I wondered if they'd mistaken me for a local politician. When I asked at school, my colleagues explained, "No, they call anyone wearing a tie guvnor."
>
> —M.H.

HARVEY NICKS

A contraction of the store name Harvey Nichols, an expensive department store that's been an icon in Knightsbridge, London, since 1880. There are also Harvey Nichols shops in other British cities.

HONKERS

Slang for someone from Hong Kong.

IRONMONGER

A hardware store. Historically, a person who deals in iron and hardware.

JANNER

A regional nickname for someone from Devon, more specifically from Plymouth.

JOCKS

People from Scotland. See **Cockney rhyming slang** page 299.

JOE BLOGGS

An "average joe" or ordinary man.

KIWI

In addition to the fruit and the bird, a Kiwi is a New Zealander.

LAUNDRETTE (LAUNDERETTE)

A laundromat.

LIMEY

American slang term for someone from Britain.

LIVERBIRD

Slang for a girl or young woman from Liverpool. The Liver Bird has also been the official symbol of Liverpool for more than eight hundred years.

MANCUNIAN, MANC

Someone from Manchester.

MARKS AND SPARKS

The nickname for Marks and Spencer, a country-wide chain of department stores. Also called "M&S."

MODS VS. ROCKERS

Mods and Rockers were two rival British youth gang-like subcultures in the early 1960s. The Mods wore smart suits, ties, and parkas and rode Italian-made scooters (Vespas or Lambrettas) equipped with as many additional chrome accoutrements as possible, while the rockers favored British motorbikes, slicked back hair, and leather jackets.

-MONGER

A vendor of something, as in "fishmonger" or "ironmonger."

MUM

Mom.

NEW AGE TRAVELERS

A subculture started in the 1960s that grew out of the free music festivals of the period. Many New Age Travelers feel a strong connection with Stonehenge. They're known for squatting in underused factories and abandoned warehouses. Bands of New Age Travelers are now in their second and third generations. Philosophically, most reject capitalism and engage in protests about the environment.

NEWSAGENT

A small shop selling newspapers, magazines, and candy.

NORMAN

A reference to the people and culture of northern France, who, led by William the Conqueror, invaded and conquered England in 1066 and formed the basis for the eventual establishment of modern England.

OAP

An Old Age Pensioner. A person receiving retirement benefits from the government.

OFF LICENSE (ALSO OFFICE AND OFFIE)

An establishment licensed to sell containers of liquor. "I'm just popping down to the offie for a bottle of red."

OFFICE WALLAH

Someone who works in an office. "Wallah" is an Indian word for worker.

PC

Police constable.

POSTMAN

A mailman or mail carrier. Also, slang "Postie."

PUNK

A subculture that began in the early 1970s in the United States with "punk rock" and took on new life in the UK in the late 1970s. It is characterized by brightly colored Mohawk hairstyles, aversion to mainstream rock-and-roll, and the rise of fanzines. The Sex Pistols were a prime example of a British punk band.

PUNTER

A customer of any business, a gambler, or a speculator. The term is also used to mean a prostitute's client, known as a "john" in the USA.

RAMBLER

A person who has a hobby of going on long walks in the countryside. There is a great tradition of rambling in the UK.

RASTA

A Rastafarian.

ROCK SCORPION

A civilian resident of Gibraltar.

SASSENACH

Person from Scotland who is ethnically English.

SCOUSER

Someone from Liverpool. The term comes from the lamb or beef stew known as "scouse" and eaten by sailors in ports like Liverpool. The terms "Plastic Scousers" and "Plazzies" refer to people who falsely claim to be from Liverpool.

SKINHEADS

Members of a youth subculture that arose in the UK in the 1960s and was eventually exported to other countries. Made up of working-class youths objecting to the status quo, in the 1980s the culture expanded with the influx of ex-punks and moved socially into neo-Fascist and neo-Nazi political views.

SLAG

A derogatory term meaning someone of loose morals.

SMOGGY

Someone from Middlesbrough in North Yorkshire.

SOLICITOR

A lawyer who is qualified to practice all areas of law but does not represent clients in court. See **Barrister** page 203.

SQUADDIE

A soldier of low rank in the British army. The word "squad" is used in the British military as a sort of blanket term for "whatever group of soldiers is around." However, the word "squaddie" became used in the early twentieth century because people were hearing the word "swaddie" and assumed they were hearing something to do with squads. A "swaddie" is an archaic English term for a lout.

SURGERY

A doctor's office, as in "the local surgery." Also widely known as the GP's (General Practitioner's) surgery. This is most like a primary care doctor's office in the Unites States. No actual surgery is done there. An "ER" (emergency room) in the United States would be called an A&E (Accident & Emergency) in the UK. See **Casualty** page 45.

TA

Territorial Army (now superseded by Army Reserve), roughly the British equivalent of the American National Guard.

TAFF (TAFFY)

A person from Wales, although originally the term meant a person from Cardiff.

"She felt a tightness in her chest and sent for Dr. Simcox.
'What's the trouble?' he asked.
'Look out there, that's the trouble! It's so green and quiet, and it's always bloody raining.'
'That's England, Mrs. Mallard-Greene. I'm afraid there's no known cure for it.'"
—John Mortimer, *Paradise Postponed*

TAVISH

Slang for a Scot. Also a term for someone skilled at mathematics.

TEDDY BOY AND TEDDY GIRL

In the early 1950s, a fashion trend emerged where boys sporting greased ducktails dressed in tailored velvet blazers, with button-down shirts, skinny ties, and chunky suede leather shoes. Girls wore tailored jackets, rolled-up jeans, and flat shoes. They formed the teen subculture from which mods, punks, and rockers evolved.

TEUCHTER

Used by lowland Scots to refer to a Scot from the "Highlands and Islands." Sometimes applied by people from Glasgow to anyone speaking a dialect other than Glaswegian. (Pronounced "TUKE-ter.")

TRAINSPOTTER

A person, usually but not always male, who likes to watch trains, keep track of train numbers, and note all the historical details of each engine and car.

TRAVELLER

A member of a group of nomadic people hailing from a variety of cultures, two of which are Romani and Irish. Since 2002, Travellers in the UK have been designated as an ethnic group and afforded some protections under the Race Relations Act.

TWITCHER

A bird watcher, especially an overenthusiastic one.

TYKE

A person from Yorkshire, who are also known as "Yorkies."

VILLAGE SHOP

In small rural villages, there may be only one shop to serve all the needs of the community, including postal and business services, groceries, drugs, and sundries.

WPC

Woman Police Constable.

YANK

An American. This slang terminology is not necessarily insulting and is applied to any American, not necessarily one from the north.

ZEBEDEE

The wizard character in the BBC TV children's series *The Magic Roundabout* who bounces around on a spring instead of legs. This character has worked its way into the mainstream vernacular of the British. If you say, "Boing!" at bedtime to people who were kids in the 1970s, they just might reply, "Time for bed, said Zebedee!"

> "All the shop ladies called me love and most of the men called me mate. I hadn't been here twelve hours and already they loved me."
> —Bill Bryson, *Notes from a Small Island*

12.

Down the Pub

A PUB MAY BE ACCURATELY DEFINED AS A PUBLIC HOUSE FOR drinking. But it's oh, so much more! It is a social center and often the heart of many smaller communities. Today, there are more than forty thousand pubs in England, three thousand in Wales, nine hundred in Northern Ireland, and four thousand in Scotland. While a British pub is not the exact equivalent of a traditional American bar, these days it is very similar to establishments where full menus as well as full bar service are offered.

Pubs were originally owned by breweries and served alcohol—mainly beer—and bar food. Beginning in the early 1980s, these traditional watering holes began to face financial challenges. Pubs declined in number, at times rather steeply. At one stage, a pub was closing every twelve hours somewhere in the UK. Various reasons are put forward for the shrinkage, including the smoking ban of 2007 and the increasing availability of cheap alcohol in supermarkets. Now, after fifteen years of decreasing numbers, pubs are once again in growth mode. The Office of National Statistics (ONS) reports that the number of pubs in the UK is beginning to increase.

One reason pubs are making a comeback is that many have added full food menus and restyled themselves as "gastropubs." In many cases, food has supplanted alcohol as a profit stream, and gastropubs are the source of some of Britain's best food.

When I first moved to the UK, I was fascinated by the stream of church-goers who would pack up Grandma, the kids (yes, children are allowed), and the dogs (yes, dogs are allowed) and head straight out the church doors and on down to the pub. Some pubs are also inns, and many are in quaint and historic buildings. Each pub is a unique experience that locals adopt as theirs. If you really want to understand British culture, start by heading to a pub.

ALE

The Campaign for Real Ale (CAMRA) defines ale as a type of beer that is brewed without hops, using malt instead, producing a darker and sweeter drink that is about six percent alcohol. A bittering agent is usually added to balance out the sweetness of the malt and act as a preservative. These days, ale is more commonly used to mean any hand-pulled beer, usually from a cask.

BAR BORE

A regular pub customer who has his own seat and often his own tankard behind the bar.

BAR STOOL PREACHER

A pub regular who thinks he knows everything and offers advice on everything.

BITTER

A style of pale ale that varies in color from gold to dark amber, and in strength typically from three to five percent alcohol by volume. A dry, sharp-tasting ale with a strong flavor of hops. It has been described as "the national drink of England," although in recent years lagers have become more popular.

BEST BITTER

FLAT WARM
BEER OF
THE YEAR

2020

BOILERMAKER

A British beer drink consisting half of draught mild beer and half of bottled brown ale. It is not the same as the American boilermaker, which is whiskey with a beer chaser.

BLACK AND TAN

A drink consisting of stout or porter mixed with bitter or light ale.

BULLOCK'S BLOOD

A cocktail of beer and rum.

CIDER

Similar to American hard cider but usually drier. It has been a pub staple for hundreds of years and is especially associated with Devon and Cornwall.

DOWN YER NECK

A colloquialism for eating or drinking, as in "Get this down yer neck, and you'll feel better."

DRUNK

Drunk, same as in the USA! Britons have a few more terms for being drunk, including but not limited to:

- Arsehold
- Bladdered
- Half-cut
- Merry
- Monged
- Off their face
- One over the eight
- Out of sorts
- Paralytic
- Pie-eyed
- Pissed
- Plastered
- Rat-arsed
- Steaming
- Sloshed
- Soused
- Sozzled
- Squiffy
- Stocious
- Tight
- Tippled
- Troattered
- Wankered

EARLY DOORS

Pubs in the UK used to be required to close in the afternoon but could reopen in the evening. "Early doors" was the name applied to those patrons who were waiting outside for the pub to reopen.

FREEHOUSE

A pub not owned by, or tied to, a brewery. It is free to sell any libations it wishes. Independently owned pubs are increasing in number.

HALF

Half a pint. "I'll have a half of London Pride please."

INGLENOOK

A very large fireplace. Inglenooks are often found in pubs and have seating on the sides, where one or two people can sit close to the fire.

> "I've never been thrown out of a pub, but I've fallen into quite a few."
>
> —Benny Bellamacina, *Philosophical Uplifting Quotes and Poems*

IPA

India Pale Ale. Beer developed in the 1780s and brewed in England for the British Empire in India, where it was too hot for brewing. IPA aged on the six-month sea voyage from England, and its flavor improved greatly during the trip. As in the USA, IPA is enjoying a huge resurgence, with craft breweries introducing new IPAs every day.

LAGER

A type of beer that is pale in color and usually has lots of bubbles. Pale lager is the most widely consumed and commercially available style of beer in the world.

LAGER AND LIME

Lager beer with a shot of lime cordial (e.g., Rose's Lime Juice) added. See **Shandy** page 226.

LAGER LOUT

Slang for a drunken, uncouth male.

LANDLORD

Most commonly refers to the proprietor of a pub but also refers to a person who leases property to tenants.

LEMONADE

A very sweet and fizzy lemon-lime soft drink. Used as a mixer in bars. Not the same as American lemonade. See **Shandy** page 226.

"They [the British] are like their own beer, froth on top, dregs at bottom, the middle excellent.

—Voltaire

LIFFEY WATER

British and Irish slang for Guinness stout.

LOCK-IN

An after-hours drinking session at a public house, technically by invitation only.

LONDON PRIDE

A tawny-colored ale brewed to 4.1 percent alcohol by Fuller's Griffin Brewery in London since the 1950s. In 2019, Fuller PLC was sold to the Japanese brewery Asahi.

MOTHER'S RUIN

A nickname for gin because in the mid-eighteenth century, the effects of gin on the family and economy were disastrous. There were around seven thousand legal gin shops in London alone, and untold numbers of illegal ones. Once considered the poor man's drink because it was so cheap, in recent years it has enjoyed a resurgence in popularity with new, so-called artisan or small-batch gins turning up in bars and on supermarket shelves.

PISSED

To be very drunk. Confusion—or laughter—ensues when an angry American says, "I'm so pissed." See **Drunk** page 222.

PLASTERED

Very drunk. See **Drunk** page 222.

"I used to have to attend meetings in London on a regular basis. On one early trip, members of my team, who were mostly British, were chatting before the meeting. One colleague was humorously telling how he 'was so pissed last night.' I listened for a while, unclear of what he was saying. 'James,' I said, 'I don't understand, why were you so angry?' 'No, no,' he replied, 'I was drinking too much and became a bit squiffy, drunk, you know, pissed.'

—Cindy Stockell

PLONK

Cheap, low-quality wine. Believed to be a corruption of *blanc*, the French word for white. Despite the reference to the color white, the term is not limited to white wine and can as easily indicate a red wine.

PUBLICAN

A person who owns or manages a pub. See **Landlord** page 224.

SCRUMPY

A strong alcoholic cider made from apples. Normally associated with southwest England, it has a cloudy appearance and dry taste. A good scrumpy normally has an alcohol content of at least seven percent by volume.

SHANDY

A drink made by mixing equal parts of beer and English (not American-style) lemonade.

SNUG

A small room in a pub, usually less open than in the public bar area. Generally, snugs hold fewer than twenty-five people.

SQUASH (ORANGE SQUASH)

A very sweet orange drink concentrate. One common brand is Robinsons.

ST CLEMENTS

A non-alcoholic drink made of orange juice mixed with bitter lemon. The drink refers to the British nursery rhyme, "Oranges and lemons, say the bells of St Clements." Very refreshing on a hot summer day.

STOUT

A strong dark beer. The most common variety is dry stout, as exemplified by Guinness Draught, the world's best-selling stout.

TROLLIED

See **Pissed** page 222.

"When the sun is out on a summer weekday afternoon, work can often take second place to a pint at the pub, standing outside, face turned towards the sun."
—Observation by an American study abroad student

13.

Wardrobe

I F YOU WANT TO RUFFLE THE FEATHERS OF A BRITISH PERSON, just remark that the UK is becoming the fifty-first state. I guarantee that it will draw a response. While the suggestion of UK statehood remains ludicrous, no one can deny the impact of American businesses on British culture. Nowhere is this influence more apparent than fast food and fast fashion. In years gone by, it was quite easy to spot an American in a train car or walking down the High Street. They were the ones wearing tennis shoes, comfortable jeans, and colorful tops. In the hot summers, they were wearing shorts.

American spotting has become more difficult in recent decades with the arrival on UK shores of Gap, American Eagle, Timberland, and North Face. American sneakers have become fashionable must-haves, and Walmart's acquisition of the Asda chain of stores has introduced the UK to George-branded clothing. Ironically, the George brand, named for its creator, George Davies, started in the UK. It was exported to the United States when Walmart bought Asda and then reintroduced it to the UK.

Although the United Kingdom adopted the metric system years ago, shirt, jacket, suit, trousers, and jean sizes are all in inches. Generally, women's sizes in the UK are two sizes larger than those in the USA except for shoes. These charts show some of the common sizes in use in the UK:

Women's Clothing Sizes		
UK Sizes		USA Sizes
XS	4	1
	6	2
S	8	4
	10	6
M	12	8
	14	10
L	16	12
	18	14
XL	20	16
	22	18
XXL	24	20
	26	22

Men's Clothing Sizes	
UK Sizes	USA Chest
XXS	32-34 ins.
XS	34-36 ins.
S	36-38 ins.
M	38-40 ins.
L	40-42 ins.
XL	42-44 ins.
XXL	44-50 ins.

Although these charts help in understanding sizes, terminology is important, too.

ANORAK

A short waist-length waterproof coat, usually with a hood. The word "anorak" is also used as a slang term for a nerdy person.

BALACLAVA

A ski mask. I always used to get this mixed up with the Greek dessert *baklava*. A knitted woolen head covering that covers your whole head with an opening for the eyes or, in three-hole models, two for the eyes and one for the mouth. A must-have accessory for skiers, bank robbers, and serial killers. The term comes from use by British troops needing to keep warm during the Crimean War, including the Battle of Balaclava.

BARBOUR

A long waterproof jacket made by J. Barbour & Sons, Ltd. Usually green, worn in the country, and supposedly thorn proof. The name Barbour refers specifically to the original wax jacket, but the company now makes a range of clothing, footwear, and accessories.

BEST BIB AND TUCKER

A person's finest clothes.

231

BOILER SUIT

An all-in-one coverall that protects clothes from oil and filth in dirty working conditions. Originally used by men working in boiler rooms.

BOOB TUBE

A tube top. A stretchy, strapless garment that covers the bust without a bra underneath. In the USA, it's a slang term for a TV.

BOWLER HAT

A black felt hat with a narrow brim and a rounded, hard top. Worn in the past by British businessmen. In America, this type of hat is known as a "derby."

BRACES

Suspenders used to hold up pants (trousers). Note that both "pants" and "suspenders" have different meanings in the UK. See **Pants** page 237 and **Suspenders** page 239.

BROTHEL CREEPERS

Shoes with thick crepe soles.

BUM BAG

A fanny pack or small bag worn around the waist that rests on top of the buttocks. In British English, "bum" is a commonly used word for "bottom," whereas "fanny" is a slightly vulgar word for "female genitalia." See **Fanny** page 292.

CAGOULE

This French-derived word (*cagoule* means "hood" in French) describes a lightweight, hooded, water-resistant coat, usually reserved for rainy days. (Pronounced "kuh-GOOL.")

CARDIE

A cardigan—a sweater with buttons down the front like a shirt.

CHEESE CUTTER

See **Flat cap** page 234.

DAPPER

Well-dressed, well to-do, or both.

DEERSTALKER

Also called "fore-and-after," a close-fitting woolen cap used for hunting and having a visor in both the front and in the back, with earflaps usually turned up and tied on top of the crown. Made of cloth, usually tweed, and often associated with Sherlock Holmes.

DINNER JACKET

A tuxedo.

DOC MARTENS

Often shortened to "Docs" or "DMs," these are the instantly recognizable high-top, lace-up boots with yellow stitching, favored by punks and skinheads. The company is headquartered in Northamptonshire.

DRESSING GOWN

A bathrobe.

DUNGAREES

Bib overalls. Denim is the most commonly used material, but dungarees can be made of pretty much any material. "Dungaree" refers to the bib component of the garment, so you might see dungaree dresses, too.

FLAT CAP

A man's cap made of wool, tweed, or other soft material. Traditionally working-class headwear from Ireland, the style has today been adopted by the young and trendy. The recent TV series *Peaky Blinders* has helped make it fashionable. Sometimes called a "Cheese cutter."

FLEECE

> A short jacket or pullover made of soft artificial material. Very useful for those damp and cold British winters—and springs, summers, and autumns!

FROCK

> A dress. Generally only used by older people. Your "posh frock" would be your best dress.

FROCK COAT

> A formal man's coat that flares out from the waist to below the knee. Popular in the Victorian and Edwardian eras, it is rarely seen these days except as part of a military uniform. Prince Harry wore a frock coat at his wedding to Meghan Markle. Hassidic Jews also often wear frock coats.

HARRIS TWEED

> A thick tweed fabric made by residents of Harris, an island in the Outer Hebrides of Scotland. Used primarily to make outerwear, dress jackets, caps, and scarves. The name is a registered trademark.

JERSEY

> As well as the name of an independent British Crown Dependency island near France, it is the term for a pullover sweater.

JIM-JAMS

> Slang for pajamas (spelled "pyjamas" in the UK).

JUMPER
A sweater.

KECKS
An informal word for trousers. Equivalent to "pants" in the USA, but don't forget that in the UK, "pants" are underwear.

KINKY BOOTS
Women's knee- or thigh-high leather boots.

KIT
The uniform and paraphernalia for a game or profession. Sometimes used generically for clothing, as in "Get your kit on, it's time to go," or "Get your kit off, I'm feeling randy."

KNICKERS
Panties or feminine underpants. The common British phrase "Don't get your knickers in a twist" has been imported to the USA as "Don't get your panties in a bunch."

LACES
Shoelaces.

MAC
A raincoat. It's short for "Mackintosh," a raincoat manufactured by a two hundred-year-old British coat maker. It's now a generic term for a raincoat. "It's looks like rain, so don't forget your mac!"

MUFFLER

A big fluffy scarf worn around the neck for warmth. There is debate about whether the scarf ceases to be a muffler once its unwrapped from the neck.

MUFTI

An old army term for non-military clothing. In schools, "free dress" days are called "mufti days."

ONESIE

Originally a piece of clothing for a baby that covered the entire body. Recently, however, similar items of clothing have become popular as pajamas or "house wear." These usually cover the arms and legs and sometimes may include slipper-like feet and even a hood. "She came down to breakfast wearing her onesie and was still wearing it at lunchtime."

PANTS

Underpants. In the UK, "pants" are worn on the inside. This term may also mean something really terrible or unattractive. "That's really pants!"

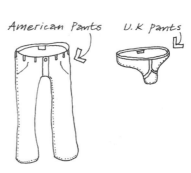

American Pants   U.K pants

PLIMSOLLS

Canvas shoes with a rubber sole, often used as school gym shoes. Sometimes referred to as "sand shoes," they may or may not have laces.

PINAFORE

Also called a "pinny," a sleeveless dress often worn over other clothes. It may also be called a "tabard." In the USA, this garment might be called a "jumper."

PORK PIE HAT

A flat-topped, round, men's hat popular with musicians of jazz, blues, and ska. Made famous by the actor Buster Keaton and the jazz musician Lester Young. Its name derives from the hat's similarity in appearance to a traditional pork pie.

PUMPS

Slang for tennis shoes.

SCHOOL UNIFORM

A standardized and required set of clothing that primary and secondary students wear to school. The uniform style is set by the school and usually consists of dark trousers or a skirt, a light colored shirt, a tie, and a blazer. Uniforms are supplied through local clothing stores.

SHREDDIES

Slang for revolting and ragged men's underwear.

SINGLET

A sleeveless athletic shirt or tank top, worn by British men as an undershirt and known by the slang term "wifebeater" in the USA. The term is falling out of use. See **Vest** page 240.

SMALLS

Underwear.

SUITED AND BOOTED

Dressed smartly.

SUSPENDERS

Small fasteners that connect a woman's hosiery to her garter belt. They *do not* hold up a man's trousers. See **Braces** page 232.

> I was a young professor at The American College in London, and newly arrived in London. Over Christmas, my girlfriend had given me a new pair of what Americans call suspenders—a beautiful pair made of shiny, black leather. I was quite pleased with them. Back in school the following January, I proudly announced to my class, "Look, I'm wearing Marion's suspenders that she gave me for Christmas!" The class instantly fell silent and then began to laugh riotously as they realized that I had no idea what I'd just said.
>
> —M.H.

SWIMMING COSTUME

A bathing suit. Also informally called a "cozzy."

TABARD

An outer garment worn by employees in retail and food
establishments for hygiene purposes.

TIGHTS

Pantyhose. They can be sheer or completely opaque.

TRAINERS

Tennis shoes or running shoes.

TRILBY

Sometimes called a "brown trilby," a fedora with a hat band
or ribbon, a pinched and indented crown, and a narrow brim.

TROLLEYS

Northern British slang for underpants.

TROUSERS

Slacks, pants. See **Pants** page 237.

TURN-UPS

Cuffs, but only the ones at the bottom of trouser legs.
British long-sleeved shirts have cuffs at the wrist.

VEST

A tee shirt, often without sleeves; undershirt.

WAISTCOAT

Vest. Usually wort with a suit.

WARDROBE

A standalone piece of furniture in the bedroom, used to keep clothing in.

WATERPROOF

A rain-resistant coat or jacket, usually hooded.

WINDCHEATER

A windbreaker.

WELLIES

Wellington boots. Named after the Duke of Wellington, they are pull-on rubber boots with a fabric lining. They're normally knee-high but can be shorter. They're usually green.

WINKLE-PICKERS

Slang for shoes with pointed toes.

Y-FRONTS

Men's briefs or "tighty whities."

14.

In and Around London

L ONDON IS A TRULY GREAT CITY, AND I HAVE CHOSEN TO MAKE it my permanent home. London is a huge amalgamation of small villages, towns, and cities, each maintaining its own characteristics, history, and identity.

A wonderful—and often bewildering—array of places to visit, food to eat, things to do, and history to see makes living in London a constant adventure. It's impossible to be bored in London, and one of my favorite activities is showing American friends around.

Here are some statistics about Americans visiting the UK:

- Around five million Americans travel to the UK every year, and nearly three-quarters of them begin their visit in London.
- New York and California generate the most visits, with the two states representing over a third of all visits from the USA to the UK.
- Nearly six out of ten American holiday visitors are making a repeat visit.
- Holiday visits are the dominant reason for an American visit.
- Most Americans who visit the UK do so during the summer.

- There are thirty-six airports in the USA that have direct flights to the UK.

Since most American visitors start their visit in London, I'll begin this section with a few tips and observations:

- Don't drive in London if you can possibly avoid it. Parking is impossible, even if you know what you're doing, and public transportation is great.
- Buy an Oyster card, and take the Tube.
- The difference between good fish and chips and bad fish and chips is like night and day. Don't give up on fish and chips until you've experienced good ones.
- Don't think you can see all the sights in two days. Consider allowing a few extra days before taking off to the countryside.
- Find a bus route that uses the new Routemaster double-decker bus, and sit upstairs. It's a great and inexpensive way to sightsee. Alternatively, take the heritage Routemaster bus. See **Routemaster** bus page 261.

Airports

There are six major airports that serve London. Most are located around the perimeter of London, with Heathrow being the closest to the center. All are connected to the city via train. Gatwick, Heathrow, and Stansted have express train service into central London.

- London City (LCY)—Known primarily as a business airport because of its accessibility to the financial district, London City Airport is located in East London but connected by Tube to central London.

- London Gatwick (LGW) —Located twenty-nine miles south of London, for many years this has been London's second airport, and many Americans land here. It is connected by rail services and the Gatwick Express to London Victoria Station.
- London Heathrow (LHR)—Heathrow is the airport that Americans are most familiar with. It is connected by Tube, rail services, and the Heathrow Express to Paddington Station.
- London Luton (LTN)—This airport is located twenty-eight miles north of London and accommodates budget airlines, charter flights, and package holiday tour operators. It is home to EasyJet. Luton is connected to central London by rail and bus services.
- London Southend (SEN)—Located in the town of Southend-on-Sea, thirty-six miles from central London, this regional airport is the most distant from London. It is connected by rail services to Liverpool Street Station.
- London Stansted (STN)—Forty-two miles to the northeast of London up the M-1 motorway, this airport serves European routes and several package tour operators. It is connected by rail services and the Stansted Express to Liverpool Street Station.

BIG BEN

The massive thirteen-ton bell in the Elizabeth Tower at the Houses of Parliament. Big Ben first rang across Westminster on May 31, 1859, and has rarely stopped, even after a bomb destroyed the Commons chamber during the

Second World War. The clock tower survived, and Big Ben continues to strike the hours today. Big Ben's timekeeping is strictly regulated by a stack of coins placed on the huge pendulum. Many tourists think that Big Ben is the name of the clock or the tower, but you'll impress your London friends if you know it is the bell only.

BRICK LANE

When I first moved to London, Brick Lane was a bit down on its luck, a street that you visited for a cheap Indian meal. In recent years, it has become a trendy alternative destination for those seeking a less structured lifestyle. This street in the Shoreditch area dates back approximately 450 years with an interesting history, first as a center for beer brewing (the Truman Brewery building can still be seen), then as a Jewish garment district, then as a community for Bengali immigrants. It is still a popular place for great Indian food, graffiti street art, Sunday flea markets, and night clubs. Added to the mix are vintage clothing shops and arts and craft markets, all of which make the street very diverse. There's something for everyone!

CAMDEN TOWN

This historic area of near north London is known for its acres of open air and covered markets centered around Camden Lock on the Grand Union Canal. There are also many international restaurants and food stalls, live music, and book shops. *Time Out* magazine describes the buzz of the area's hippie vibe as having "an unorthodox charm." Use Camden Town Tube station or Chalk Farm Tube station.

> "Visitors to British hotels will soon realize that *Fawlty Towers* was really a documentary."
> —Lonely Planet's *Great Britain*

CHARING CROSS

This is the name of the road junction just to the south of Trafalgar Square. The cross that sits in front of Charing Cross station is the point from which all distances to London are measured. So, if you see a road sign that says 42 miles to London, it means 42 miles to Charing Cross.

CANARY WHARF

Noted for its modern skyscrapers, this area also has green open spaces and open areas by the Thames. It also has a number of shops, bars, and restaurants. The Museum of London Docklands tells the story of this richly historic and fascinating part of London. Take the Docklands Light Railway (DLR) from Royal Victoria to West India or Canary Wharf.

CHILTERN HILLS

Although not in London proper, the Chiltern Hills are a range of chalk hills running from southwest to northeast, located to the northwest of London. This Area of Outstanding Natural Beauty (AONB) covers 324 square miles of countryside, stretching from the River Thames in southern Oxfordshire up through Buckinghamshire and Bedfordshire to Hitchin in Hertfordshire. At 876 feet (or 267 meters) above sea level, Haddington Hill, near Wendover, is the highest viewpoint in the Chilterns.

> "The expression 'right as rain' must have been invented by an Englishman."
>
> —William Lyon Phelps

CITY

This was traditionally the financial district of London, although many banking institutions have now moved to the Isle of Dogs. The City, also called "the Square Mile" and "the financial district," contains the Gherkin, The Bank of England, the Monument, London Guildhall, Mansion House, and the Museum of London. The local authority of the City of London Corporation is headed by the Lord Mayor of London (not the same as the Mayor of London). If you get into a taxi and ask to be taken into The City, you'll end up in the financial district.

COVENT GARDEN

This is a tourist "hot spot" in London that I want to dislike but just can't. It is a covered market with impressive architecture, surrounded by a cobblestone piazza in London's West End. Formerly the site of one of London's fruit and vegetable markets, it now contains a multitude of museums, including my favorite, the London Transport Museum. It also has high-end restaurants, shopping, and the Royal Opera House.

> "When a man is tired of London, he is tired of life; for there is in London all that life can afford."
>
> —Samuel Johnson

DLR

The Docklands Light Railway is a driverless train line that serves areas of South and East London and is connected to the London Underground network. It is a fully automated transportation system that also serves London City Airport and the Emirates Air Line Cable Car. The DLR's fares are the same as the Tube's, and you can use your Oyster card, travelcard, and contactless payment card to purchase fares. Opened in 1987 to serve the redeveloped Docklands area of East London, it has since been extended to reach Stratford to the north and Woolwich to the south.

DOCKLANDS

Formerly called the "Port of London," the Docklands is an area on the River Thames. It had been used for centuries as the primary place to unload cargo ships, warehouse the goods, and distribute them to the rest of the UK. These nine square miles have now become uber-gentrified and expensive.

EAST END

There doesn't seem to be any precise definition of where London's East End begins and ends. However, most will agree that it lies east of "the City" as far as the River Lea and includes Whitechapel, Mile End, Shoreditch, and Brick Lane. Depending on who's defining it, the Isle of Dogs and the Docklands may be included. It has long been associated with workers' residences for the Docklands, and in 1888 it gained notoriety for the murders attributed to Jack the Ripper. The area has always had a distinct cultural identity, and people from the area are known as Cockneys.

It took me a while to understand just how big a role World War II plays in the British psyche. Unlike many Americans, most British who lived through the war know how close they came to losing their country. Hitler was only twenty-six miles away in northern France.

The war is not just a distant memory of past generations. There are still plenty of people who can tell stories about sheltering in the London Underground stations while German bombers pummeled London from above. In fact, American talk show host Jerry Springer was born in the Highgate Underground station during one of those air raids.

When I first moved to the UK in the 1980s, I lived in Philbeach Gardens in Earls Court. Several houses along that street were missing, and giant buttress beams held up neighboring walls. On one remaining wall, someone had spray painted "Remodeled courtesy of A. Hitler."

More than twenty thousand bombs fell on London, destroying or damaging more than one hundred thousand buildings beyond repair. Even today, unexploded bombs

(UXBs) are sometimes found in London's East End during excavation, and construction is halted while they are defused and disposed of.

Many bomb sites in London were used as parking lots after the war. The National Car Parks (NCP) parking lot empire started with a £200 purchase of a bomb site on Red Lion Square, the first of many such purchases.

British people who lived through the war adopted a "Grow your own," "Do it yourself," "Make do and mend," and "Keep calm and carry on!" mentality that still permeates British consciousness today. People of the war generation simply did not throw anything away. The first house I bought in the UK had belonged to a family of that era. The loft was stuffed with bits of cloth, Christmas wrapping paper, old leather shoes, pads of paper, pencil stubs, pieces of wire—anything that might have some kind of future use. The garage was packed with wooden boxes full of metal scraps and objects—brass, aluminum, copper, and steel.

Rationing of some foods and fuel persisted well after the war ended, until July of 1954. It took until December of 2006 for the UK to finally finish paying off its war loan debt to the USA. British architecture, ideas about food, city planning, finances, and politics were all deeply affected by World War II, and the influence is still profound.

—M.H.

EEL PIE ISLAND

This smallish island in the River Thames near Twickenham is home to an artist community and the Twickenham Rowing Club. In the 1960s, it was known for rock concerts by the newly formed Rolling Stones, The Who, Genesis, and Pink Floyd. It became popularly known as "the place where the '60s began." It can be reached today by a narrow footbridge, but unless it's the artists' "Open Weekend," there is little to see.

ELIZABETH TOWER

The north tower of the Houses of Parliament that holds "Big Ben," the bell synonymous with the sounds of London. Formerly just called the "Clock Tower," in June of 2012, the House of Commons announced that it was to be renamed the Elizabeth Tower in honor of Queen Elizabeth II's Diamond Jubilee. Elizabeth Tower stands more than three hundred feet tall. Big Ben is the name of the bell, not the tower. The best view is from Westminster Bridge.

EMIRATES AIR LINE CABLE CAR

This is a cable car across the River Thames in London's East End between the Greenwich Peninsula and the Royal Victoria Dock near Canning Town station. The one-kilometer, ten-minute journey provides some spectacular views of London's Olympic Park, Canary Wharf, the O2 Arena, and the Thames Barrier from a height of nearly three hundred feet. At a cost of nearly £60 million, the cable car was the first to bear a commercial brand on the London Tube map and was opened in time for the 2012 London Olympics. You can use your London Oyster card just as you would on the Tube or buses. The closest station is Royal Victoria, on the DLR (Docklands Light Railway), which is about two hundred yards away. The Thames Barrier is close by and can be reached by walking along the river.

EYOT (AIT)

A small sedimentary island in a river, usually long and thin. Used traditionally in the UK to describe islets in the River Thames and its tributaries. (Both spellings are pronounced "ate.")

An American colleague explained to me once that Londoners are kind of like gophers. They ride around on the Tube all the time and only occasionally pop their heads out from underground to see what's going on. I have found this to be true. Because the Tube map is highly stylized and not related to distances or geography, we often don't appreciate the relationships among stations, especially ones on different lines. It took me several years to realize that Covent Garden station on the Piccadilly Line and Charing Cross station on the Northern Line are only three blocks apart.

—M.H.

FINANCIAL DISTRICT

See **City** page 99, page 248.

GATE

"The Gate" refers to the Notting Hill Gate district of London.

GOLDERS GREEN

Golders Green, in the north London borough of Barnet, is home to a large Orthodox Jewish community and is known as the kosher hub of London. There are also strong Southeast Asian and Japanese influences in the area. There are several Jewish temples in the area.

GREENWICH

This town on the River Thames is probably best known for being the location of the Prime Meridian and the Royal Observatory. It lends it name to Greenwich Mean Time (GMT). It is great fun to visit the observatory and straddle the Prime Meridian. This is the point from which all time zones and longitudes are measured. Observatory hill also provides some of the best views overlooking London and has appeared in many movies. The town of Greenwich is home to the Royal Naval College and Maritime Museum, designed by Sir Christopher Wren, as well as the Cutty Sark clipper ship—both worth a visit. (Pronounced "GREN-itch.")

"England is my home. London is my home. New York feels like, if I must spend a year living in an unfamiliar city, this is a lovely one to spend a year in, but I will be going home at the end of it, certainly."

—Daniel Radcliffe

GREENWICH FOOT TUNNEL

One interesting and unusual activity, especially if you're already in Greenwich, is to walk under (that's right, under!) the Thames via the Greenwich Foot Tunnel. Opened in 1902, it was intended to provide a reliable route for workers living south of the river to reach the Docklands. It has been upgraded twice in its life, most recently in 2012. The most convenient access is next to the Cutty Sark in Greenwich or via the Island Gardens Tube station on the north side. Access is free.

ISLE OF DOGS

You wouldn't know it by looking at it today, but what is now the financial hub of London was once considered wasteland and used for grazing sheep. This peninsula of land jutting southward, and defined by the River Thames, was once marshland. There are records dating to the Middle Ages of attempts to drain the area. Theories abound as to why it's called the Isle of Dogs, since it is neither an island nor is there is any record of dogs being particularly prolific there. The London Docks, established there in the early 1800s, transformed the area into "the Docklands" that today host a multitude of gleaming skyscrapers.

JUNCTION

"The Junction" is British slang for the area of London around Clapham Junction.

KNOWLEDGE

"The Knowledge" is the London taxi drivers' exam that tests their familiarity with London's streets. It's renowned for being very difficult.

LEICESTER SQUARE

A historic square located in London's West End theater district. Today, it is a tourist destination with cinemas, restaurants, novelty shops, and, of course, theaters. It was extensively redeveloped for the 2012 Olympic Games. The Odeon Cinema and Empire Cinema are often used for UK red carpet premiers of American films. (Pronounced "LESS-ter Square.")

LONDON EYE

Built for the millennium celebrations, this rotating observation wheel takes visitors nearly three hundred feet into the London sky in glass "pods" and provides fabulous

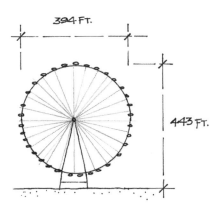

views of London. Located on the south end of Westminster Bridge.

LONDON OVERGROUND

Launched in 2007 and managed by Transport for London (TfL), this rail service provides connections between London's suburban boroughs and its major rail stations. Known generally at "the Overground," it uses the same round sign and logo as "the Underground," but its color scheme is orange. There are six lines, and an Oyster card is accepted.

M25

Americans would describe the M25 motorway as London's "outer belt," "ring road," or "beltway." It is a circular, limited-access highway running more than seventy miles around London. The M25 connects many major motorways and provides a vital way to circumnavigate the city without entering the center. It used to run through rural countryside, but today many parts of London have grown to encompass it. It is always busy, and locals will sometimes refer to it as "the UK's largest car park." It is also used in giving directions, with destinations being described as either inside or outside the M25.

To get to the American Intercontinental University every day, I had to take the Piccadilly Line from Barons Court into central London. After a couple of weeks, I began noticing that the train cars didn't travel in a straight line. In fact, they were making some sharp turns. I was told that these exist because when engineers were designing these underground railroads, they tried to avoid "plague pits," mass graves dating back to the time of the Black Death in 1348. Supposedly, they didn't want to disturb the dead, or possibly the bodies were packed too thickly to bore through. It's an interesting story, but Transport for London (TfL) says it isn't backed up by any historical evidence and is probably an urban myth. In reality, the curves are there because of geology or because the train company couldn't acquire the right of way.

—M.H.

MARKETS

In the introduction to this section, I mentioned that London is a great amalgamation of many smaller villages, towns, and cities, each maintaining its own characteristics, history, and identity. This is particularly manifest in the hundreds of local markets that spring up every day of the week and especially on the weekends. Some markets, such as Borough, Covent Garden, and Brixton Markets, are permanent fixtures in their communities. Everything imaginable is for sale, from antiques, old junk, art, and jewelry to vegetables, prepared food, and specialty gift items. Here is just a partial list. It doesn't really do justice to the local market scene, but it's a good place to start.

- Alexandra Palace Farmer's Market—Wood Green
- Billingsgate Fish Market—Billingsgate
- Borough Market—London Bridge
- Brick Lane Market—Shoreditch
- Brixton Market—Brixton
- Broadway Market—Hackney
- Camden Lock Market—Camden
- Columbia Road Flower Market—Bethnal Green
- Covent Garden—Covent Garden
- Greenwich Market—Greenwich Cutty Sark
- Herne Hill Market—Herne Hill
- Ladbroke Grove Farmer's Market—Ladbroke Grove
- Maltby Street Market—Bermondsey
- Old Spitalfields Market—Farringdon
- Petticoat Lane—Spitalfields
- Portobello Road Market—Notting Hill

- Southbank Book Market—Waterloo
- Victoria Park Market—Cambridge Heath

MISERY LINE

The Northern Line that crosses London from the northeast to the southwest has two branches and travels through Euston Station. It is a "deep level" line, which means it is expensive to maintain. It has also been denied crucial funding for maintenance and improvement. Not surprisingly, the line developed a reputation for signal failures, train breakdowns, and general unreliability. When *The Evening Standard* newspaper began calling the Northern Line "the Misery Line," the name stuck. In recent years, better funding has improved reliability, along with increased willingness by Transport for London (TfL) to develop long-term solutions.

OLD BAILEY

The buildings located outside the western wall of medieval London that contain the central criminal courts in London. Seen and discussed in multitudes of police and judicial television shows.

OYSTER CARD

A Transport for London travel card that allows you to pre-pay and then debit the card for each journey traveled. With an Oyster card, there's no waiting in line to purchase individual tickets. Additionally, it saves money and it never expires. You can save it for a future visit or pass it along to a friend. An Oyster card works on buses, the Tube, trams, the Docklands Light Railway (DLR), and the London Overground. It's also good for travel to and from both Gatwick and Heathrow airports.

PEARLY KINGS AND QUEENS

Charity fundraisers who wear clothing decorated all over with pearl buttons. The origin of the practice is associated with Henry Croft, who collected money for charity and wanted to draw attention to his cause. Eventually, the tradition was adopted by other charity fundraisers, who became known as the "Pearlies."

PILLAR BOX

A tall, old-fashioned mailbox that stands alone like a pillar. Each box bears the initials of the reigning monarch at the time the box was installed. There are one or two still in use that carry the initials VR, which stand for "Victoria Regina."

RICHMOND

A lovely town on the southwest side of London on the upper reaches of the River Thames. This area has long been a summer retreat for royalty and the rich and famous. Hampton Court Palace is a few minutes away by train, and Kew Botanical Gardens are nearby. Richmond Park is a Royal Park of more than 2,500 acres and boasts a large herd of wild deer. Dwight D. Eisenhower stayed in Thatched House Lodge in Richmond Park during preparations for the D-Day landings of World War II. The walk along the riverfront is what most visitors remember.

> "You can just about tell the month of the year by the length of the lines outside Madame Tussauds."
> —An American expat living in London

ROUTEMASTER BUS

The iconic red double-decker Routemaster bus ranks up there with phone boxes and the Houses of Parliament among things to photograph in London. Routemasters began their run in London in 1956 and remained in use for forty-nine years until they were withdrawn from service in 2005. Many were purchased privately and converted to sightseeing buses. One heritage route, #15H, still survives. Running alongside the regular new Routemaster buses, the old-style vehicles start at the Tower Hill bus stop and run to Trafalgar Square in twenty-minute intervals Monday through Friday. They still allow passengers to "hop on and hop off." Because of their enduring popularity, new Routemaster buses were introduced in 2012 as part of a flagship project by Boris Johnson when he was mayor of London.

SHOREDITCH

As a part of historic East London, Shoreditch lies immediately north of the City of London in the borough of Hackney. For many centuries, the focal point of Shoreditch was its church, which is mentioned in a couplet in the nursery rhyme "Oranges and Lemons." There are at least a dozen theories about how Shoreditch got its name, but historians believe that the word "shoreditch" comes from water that ran across the area's marshland. It was originally known as Soersditch, or Sewer's Ditch.

SMOKE

"The smoke" is a slang nickname for London.

SOHO

An area of central London known for its nightlife. In the 1960s, it was a less-than-salubrious destination for those seeking sexual encounters and down-market entertainment. It is known today for its nightclubs, theaters, and restaurants although seedy parts still exist. Officially part of the West End, it is bordered on the south by Piccadilly Circus and Shaftsbury Avenue, Oxford Street to the north, and Regent Street to the west.

> "To park your car for an hour in Soho costs more than the minimum wage. There are people working in McDonald's in Soho who can look out of the window and see parking meters earning more than they do."
> —Simon Evans

SOUTH BANK

An area on the South Bank of the River Thames that is both a commercial and artistic center. Running along the river between Blackfriars and Westminster Bridges, the South Bank has such attractions as the National Theatre, the British Film Institute (BFI) Southbank, the London Eye, the Royal Festival Hall, and the Southbank Centre. Restaurants, street vendors, book sellers, and street entertainers define the South Bank experience. You can enjoy beautiful views of the Houses of Parliament and St Paul's Cathedral, especially in the early morning and at dusk. I suggest arriving at the Embankment Tube station and walking across the Hungerford footbridge to the south side of the river.

SOUTH OF THE RIVER

Once upon a time, this was an important distinction for visitors to London because of the notable socio-economic differences between the communities on each side of the river. We'd call this "the wrong side of the tracks" in the USA. For generations, the south side was less developed and experienced inequitable growth. This may have been in part because the Tube did not extend south of the river, and that kept property prices lower. In recent decades, and as a partial response to London's housing crisis, there have been better investment in infrastructure and improved rail and transportation links.

SQUARE MILE

A colloquial reference to the "City of London" which is just over a square mile—although it's anything but square. This local government district contains the original Roman settlement of Londinium and today much of the financial district. It also contains St Paul's Cathedral and the Barbican, but my favorite is The Old Mitre, a five hundred-year-old pub tucked away in an alley and now surrounded by much taller modern buildings. See **City** page 248.

> "The sun doesn't live in England; it comes here on holiday when we're all at work."
> —Benny Bellamacina, *Piddly Poems for Children*

ST PANCRAS INTERNATIONAL

Located on the Euston Road, St Pancras railway station has served the capital since 1868. When I first moved to London in the late 1980s, the station was a derelict shadow of its former glorious self, with broken roof glass, pigeons in residence, and trash everywhere. Still, even in that sad state, you could see that once it had been a shining example of Victorian architecture and brickwork turned into an art form. In 1966, British Railways announced that it intended to amalgamate St Pancras and nearby King's Cross stations and eliminate most of those original buildings. There was a public outcry, and Poet Laureate John Betjeman led the campaign to get St Pancras station protected as a "Grade 1 listed" building. The campaign was successful, and renovation of the structure began in 2003.

Today, it is known officially as St Pancras International, since it is the London home of the Eurostar services to the continent and hosts a multitude of trendy shopping and eating establishments. It is well worth a visit, even if you're not travelling.

> "On the Continent, people have good food; in England, people have good table manners."
>
> —George Mikes

STRAND

The Strand is a street in London that runs from Trafalgar Square eastward to Fleet Street, a distance of about three-quarters of a mile. It runs roughly parallel to the River Thames and once served as the main route connecting the City of Westminster and the City of London. It's a popular commercial district with many famous businesses, including Twinings Tea's original shop, Simpsons-on-the-Strand restaurant, and three theaters. Covent Garden is nearby. The street derives its name from the Old English word meaning "bank" or "shore," because for many decades it was the road closest to the bank of the river. Today, the bank of the river has been reinforced (The Embankment), and The Strand is several hundred yards inland.

STRATFORD

This is an area of London, not to be confused with Stratford-upon-Avon. It is located seven miles northeast of central London in the borough of Newham and was the site of the

2012 London Olympics. Formerly an underdeveloped and undesirable area, the London Olympics and the creation of the huge Westfield Shopping Complex a few years later have made Stratford a much more desirable place to live. Visit the Queen Elizabeth Olympic Park, or for a drive-by glimpse, take the Stratford International on the Docklands Light Railway from Royal Victoria Station. Leaving Stratford, sit on the left side of the train for the best view.

THAMES BARRIER

Spanning 1706 feet across the Thames, this is one of the world's largest flood-defense systems. Opened in 1982, it protects nearly fifty square miles of central London from the "storm surge" and tidal flooding, which regularly brought the city to a halt. Ten steel gates rise during conditions of potential flooding, then go back down once the danger has subsided. The Thames Barrier Visitor Centre on the south side of the River tells the story of the Barrier and explains how it works.

THEATER DISTRICT

Located in London's West End, the theater district is home to more than forty theatres in total. It is a tourist magnet, with many choosing to spend at least some of their time in London seeing a "West End show." The district comes alive in the evening with gourmet restaurants, neon lights, and plenty of pubs. The area is roughly defined by Piccadilly Circus to the west, Trafalgar Square to south, Tottenham

Court Road to the north, and Covent Garden to the east. Leicester Square Tube station often acts as the starting point for a visit to the theater district.

> "Definition of a Londoner: 'One who has never been to Madame Tussauds.'"
>
> —Craig Willis

TRAFALGAR SQUARE

A square in the City of Westminster with two fountains and Nelson's Column. Opened to the public in 1844, it is named after Britain's historic 1805 victory over the French at the battle of Trafalgar during which Admiral Lord Nelson was killed on his ship, *HMS Victory*. Over the years, the square has long been a place for protests, demonstrations, and large-scale events. Though once known for the thousands of pigeons that flocked there to be fed, the feeding of birds was banned in 2001. The National Portrait Gallery borders one side of the square.

TRAMS

In the year 2000, trams were introduced in parts of south London that had been underserved by the Tube network. Trams run among Wimbledon, Croydon, Beckenham, and New Addington. They are considered a part of the bus network, and Oyster cards are valid for fare payment.

TUBE

Vernacular for the "London Underground," "The Tube" is made up of eleven lines in nine zones. Central London is zone 1. The iconic Tube map shows the relationship of all 250 stations and 250 miles of track. About half is actually underground. The Tube handles over five million passenger trips each day. It is, without question, the best way for a visitor to London to get around efficiently. All major tourist destinations are served by the Tube. See **Underground** page 112.

> "Train surfing is the process of trying to keep your balance on an underground carriage when there isn't anything to hang onto."
>
> —American study-abroad student

WEST END

"The West End" refers to the theater district of London centered around Leicester Square.

ZONES

The Tube, Docklands Light Railway (DLR), London Overground, and National Rail services in London are divided into zones. Most services operate in zones 1 through 6. The Tube, London Overground, and National Rail also operate in zones 7 through 9.

15.

Place Names

AMERICANS VISITING THE UK ARE OFTEN AMUSED AND delighted by the unique and sometimes bizarre place names they discover on their travels or on the road maps. From Cow Roast in Hertfordshire to Much Wenlock in the Midlands, there is plenty to laugh at on a map of the UK. But in addition to inspiring giggles, these names often reveal a fascinating history.

The place names of Britain are the results of three thousand years of conquests, occupation, cultural influence, and trade. Prehistoric peoples were followed by the Celts, and then the Romans, Anglo-Saxons, Vikings, and Normans each had a period of influence. Even today, many geographic features in the UK have kept their Celtic place names. For example, about two-thirds of England's rivers have names of Celtic origin, including the Avon, Derwent, Severn, Tees, Trent, and Tyne. The River Itchen later lent its name to the town of Bishop's Itchington. Often, the names meant "river" or "water," and in some cases the meanings have been lost. The name of the River Thame in Buckinghamshire comes from the Celtic for "dark one" or "river," as does that of the River Thames.

The Roman invasion of AD 55 and subsequent occupation had a profound linguistic influence. Place names attributed to the Romans mainly come through the Latinization of pre-Roman words. For example, the ancient Greek name of Pretannike, the

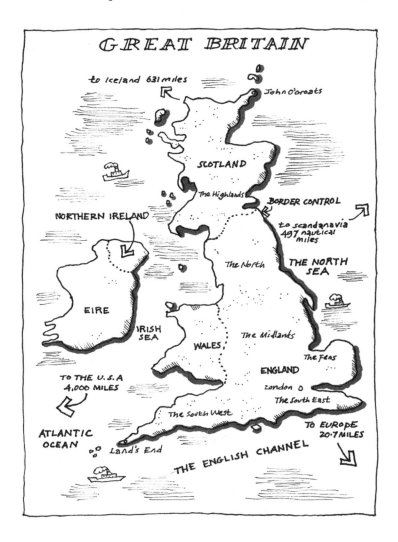

island off the northwest coast of Europe, became the Roman name Britannia. When the Vikings arrived in the eighth century via the northeast and Scotland, they named places according to the roles they played, like major farming areas or villages.

The year 1066 marked a big change in British history when the French-speaking William the Conqueror prevailed over Harold Godwinson at the Battle of Hastings. William gave farmsteads and territories to his French knights as rewards for their support. The resulting place names are lasting mementos of the Norman Invasion. The words *bois* (woods) *beau lieu* (beautiful place), and *rouge mont* (red hill) are examples. But even though French had its day, English, the language of the Anglo-Saxon natives, eventually regained its role as the language of government and rule. The result of foreign influence and English resilience is nowhere better illustrated than in the wonderful uniqueness of British place names.

-BOOTH

>A Danish suffix meaning "cattle shelter," originally "both."

-BOROUGH

>Similarly, to -bury, this is different spelling of word meaning a fortified place, e.g., Scarborough. Also -brough (e.g., Middlesbrough), -burgh (e.g., Edinburgh—where it is pronounced "burra"). Locals will sometimes abbreviate this further to "-bru."

-BOTTOM

Anglo Saxon suffix for valley. Originally "-bothm."

-BURY

An Anglo Saxon place name suffix meaning "a fortified place," as in Roxbury and Middlebury.

-BY

Meaning settlement or village, from the Old Norse. Pronounced "bee," as in Derby or Rugby.

-CESTER

A town or city established by the Romans. Originally, *castra* (meaning "fort") in Latin, in Anglo Saxon it became *ceaster*, which gradually mutated to *cester*, pronounced "sester." Examples include Bicester, Leicester, Worcester, and Gloucester. There is nothing that says "American" faster than pronouncing somewhere like Leicester as "LIE-sester." It's simply "LESS-ter," and the same goes for "BISS-ter" and "GLOSS-ter." Worcester is double-pitfall territory: it's pronounced "WUSSter." Cirencester is the biggest test of all—this one *is* pronounced in full: "SIGH-ren-sess-ter."

-FORD

A reference to a town or city where a river was traditionally crossed, e.g., Hungerford.

-HAM

A suffix meaning "farm" or "homestead," as in Buckingham or Durham. It comes from a word meaning "home."

HRYTHER-

Anglo-Saxon for "horned cattle." Often seen used in the form of "Rother," as in the names Rotherwick and Rotherham.

-INGS

A shortened version of the Anglo-Saxon suffix "-ingas," indicating the lineage and followers of a specific family. One example is Hastings, which originally identified the area settled by the Haestas family.

LIVER-

An Anglo-Saxon prefix meaning "muddy water," as in Liverpool.

-LY, -LAY, -LEY, AND -LEIGH

Old English for "a clearing in a wood," usually associated with a farming community. Examples include Stoneleigh, Leigh Place, and Henley.

-MERE

Anglo Saxon for "lake," as in Windemere.

-MOUTH

A reference to a town or city located at the mouth of a river. The first part of the town's name was usually the name of the river. For example, Plymouth on the river Ply. When used as a suffix, it's pronounced "muth."

MUCH

Comes from the Anglo-Saxon "*mycel*," meaning "great" or "much." Examples include Much Birch and Much Wenlock.

-THONG

Anglo-Saxon for a narrow strip of land. One example is Netherthong.

-THORPE

From the Middle English "thorp," meaning village, now spelled with an extra "e" on the end as in Scunthorpe.

-THWAITE

From the archaic Danish "thwait," meaning "clearing or meadow." Spelled today with an "e" at the end, as in Bassenthwaite and Crossthwaite.

-TOFT

An old Danish suffix meaning "homestead." Examples include Wistoft, Langtoft, and Lowestoft.

-TON

Anglo-Saxon for "enclosed village" or "farmstead." Examples include Brighton and Everton.

-TRY

>Anglo-Saxon for "tree." Examples include Coventry and Daventry.

-WICK, -WICH

>From an Anglo-Saxon suffix meaning "farm." Examples include Norwich, Greenwich, Warwick, and Hacney Wick in London.

-WOLD

>From an Anglo-Saxon for "forest." Also sometimes called "weald" or "wald." Examples include Cotswolds, Stow-on-the-Wold, Wealdstone, and North Weald.

-WORTH

>Old English for "enclosure." Examples include Letchworth and Tamworth.

Humorous and Rude Place Names in England
- Beaver Close, Surrey
- Bell End near Lickey End, Worcestershire
- Brown Willy, Cornwall
- Cock Lane in Tutts Clump, Berkshire
- Cockplay, Northumberland
- Crotch Crescent, Oxford
- Dicks Mount, Suffolk
- Fanny Hands Lane, Lincolnshire
- Fudgepack upon Humber, Humberside
- Grope Lane, Shropshire

- Honey Knob Hill, Wiltshire
- Lickers Lane, Merseyside
- Menlove Avenue, Liverpool
- Piddle River, Dorset
- Prickwillow, Cambridgeshire
- Scratchy Bottom, Dorset
- Spanker Lane, Derbyshire
- Stow cum Quy, Cambridgeshire
- Titty Hill, Sussex
- Turkey Cock Lane, Colchester, Essex
- Upper Dicker and Lower Dicker, East Sussex

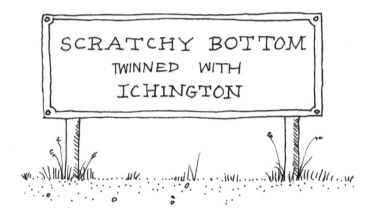

Humorous and Rude Place Names in Scotland
- Butt of Lewis, Hebrides
- Cock of Arran, Isle of Arran
- Forest Dyke Road, Lanarkshire
- The Bastard (mountain), Knapdale and Kintyre
- Twatt, Orkney

Humorous and Rude Welsh Place Names

- Bullyhole Bottom, Monmouthshire
- Sodom, Flintshire
- Stop-and-Call, Pembrokeshire
- Tarts Hill, Flintshire, Wales
- Three Cocks, Breconshire

Humorous and Rude Northern Ireland Place Names

- Craigadick, Derry
- Cum, Mayo
- Doodys Bottoms, Wicklow
- Hackballs Cross, Louth
- Lousybush, Kilkenny
- Muff, Donegal

16.

Politics, Titles and the "Realm"

MANY AMERICANS ARE FASCINATED THAT ENGLAND HAS A queen, a royal family, and inherited titles. Perhaps it's because they contrast so greatly with the egalitarian and Horatio Alger ideals that are so much a part of American culture. I've recently heard the royal family described by Americans as being "cute," a description usually reserved for describing teddy bears and farmyard animals. It's quite unlikely that you will hear a Brit describe royalty thus.

In case you're invited to a dinner party in the UK where the topic erupts into conversation about royalty, here is a quick cheat list:

The Peerage system, the British aristocracy by rank

- The Monarch: The queen or king.
- The Queen Consort: The wife of a ruling king. (The world will know the holder of this title as the queen, but technically she is the queen consort.)

- The Prince Consort: The husband of a ruling queen. (Philip is prince consort, because he is married to Queen Elizabeth.)
- Prince/Princess: A child of the monarch, or a title inherited from a parent who is a prince or princess.
- Duke/Duchess: The highest level of British peerage (Level 1)
- Marquess (Pronounced "MAR-kwess")/Marchioness (Pronounced "MAR-shuh-ness" (Level 2)
- Earl/Countess (Level 3)
- Viscount (Pronounced "VIE-count")/Viscountess (VIE-count-ess") (Level 4)
- Lord/Lady: Those at levels 2, 3 and 4 may be referred to as "Lord" or "Lady" (with their first name) instead of by their full title, as may their children.
- Baron: (Level 5)
- Baronet/Baronetess: A baron is a member of a British hereditary dignity made up of commoners. It is an order of honor, ranking below a baron but above all knights except those of the Garter (an order of knighthood appointed by the monarch). The title is designated by the word "Sir" before the name and "Baronet" after. When a baronet dies, the title is passed on to his son. The baronetage is not part of the peerage, nor is it an order of knighthood.
- Knight/Life Peer: An honor given to individuals. They are awarded the title of Sir or Dame.

Barons, viscounts, earls, marquesses, and their female counterparts may all be referred to as "Lord" or "Lady," instead of their full title, as may their children.

COMMONWEALTH

Formed in 1926, the Commonwealth (formerly the British Commonwealth of Nations) is an association of nations consisting of the United Kingdom and more than forty former British colonies that are now sovereign states but have chosen to maintain ties of friendship and practical cooperation. Since 1949, membership has been open to nations without any colonial history with the UK. Membership today is based on free and equal voluntary co-operation. The last two countries to join the Commonwealth, Rwanda and Mozambique, have no historical ties to the British Empire. Canada, Australia, and New Zealand are members of the Commonwealth.

> "The English lord marries for love and is rather inclined to love where the money is."
> —Nancy Mitford

COUNCIL

The local governmental body that provides public services such as trash collection, social services, and fire protection. All British citizens pay local council taxes in addition to their national income tax.

ENGLAND

The country of England, not including Scotland or Wales. The three countries together form Great Britain. The United Kingdom is formed of these countries plus Northern Ireland. People from any of the four may be referred to as "British" (although many will choose to identify as their own nationality (i.e., English, Welsh, Scottish, or Northern Irish).

> "There's as much chance of my becoming prime minister as there is of finding Elvis on Mars, or my being decapitated by a frisbee or reincarnated as an olive!"
> —Boris Johnson

HOUSE OF COMMONS

One of the two parts of Parliament in the UK, the other being the non-elected House of Lords. The house is made up of 650 elected members known as "Members of Parliament" or "MPs." Each represents a particular area of the country.

HOUSE OF LORDS

One of the two parts of Parliament in the UK, the other being the elected House of Commons. Members of the House of Lords are appointed by the Queen on the advice of the Prime Minister. Currently, there are about eight hundred members who are eligible to take part in the work of the House of Lords. Historically, this body was composed of life or hereditary peers and bishops. In 1999, most were replaced by political appointees, and there is continuing debate as to how the House of Lords could be reformed to be composed more democratically.

HUNDRED

An old administrative division subdividing the traditional county or "shire." This term was replaced by "district" in 1894, but "hundred" still shows up on some modern maps.

JEWEL IN THE CROWN

During the time of the extended British Empire, upon which "the sun never set," India was commonly thought of as the jewel in the crown of colonial holdings.

LADY

A woman from an upper social class in the UK. A formal form of address in the UK, "Lady" is used before the family name of a woman with a noble title.

LORD

A title used in front of the names of male peers and officials of very high rank. In Britain, judges, bishops, and some male members of the nobility are addressed as "My Lord."

> "Nobody seemed quite clear whether the expression 'drunk as a lord' should be taken as a compliment or an insult."
> —Lord Stormont Mancroft

LORD MAYOR OF LONDON

The role of the Lord Mayor of London is not be confused with that of the Mayor of London. The Lord Mayor serves for a one-year term of office and is apolitical. He presides over the City of London's governing bodies and is head of the City of London Corporation. He plays a key role in promoting UK-based financial services and related business services, both nationally and internationally. He presides over an annual parade through the City of London. The Mayor of London, on the other hand, serves a four-year term and is the chief administrator of the city, overseeing fire, police, and transportation services as well as economic development in the Greater London area.

> "The House of Lords is good evidence of life after death."
> —Baron Soper

MARQUESS

A male member of the nobility who has a rank between Duke and Earl. In French, it is spelled "Marquis." (Pronounced MAR-kwess.")

MEP

Member of European Parliament. As of January 2020, there are no longer any MEPs representing the UK.

MP

Member of Parliament.

NATIONAL INSURANCE NUMBER

The equivalent of a social security number, the unique personal identification number used for distributing state benefits and collecting taxes.

NATIONAL TRUST

The National Trust for Places of Historic Interest or Natural Beauty. This private organization owns and manages many of the country houses and mansions that were formerly the estates of the landed gentry in England. Funded through donations, the National Trust also preserves delicate coastline and wildlife areas.

NHS

The National Health Service.

OBE

The Order of the British Empire. An order of chivalry that rewards contributions to the arts and sciences.

PEER

A Peer of the Realm, a member of the highest aristocratic social order, second only to the royal family.

RAJ

Commonly called the "British Raj," this was the period between 1858 and 1947, when the Indian subcontinent was subject to British Crown rule.

REALM

"The Realm" refers to the British Empire, including a worldwide network of colonies, protectorates, and other territories that, over a span of some three centuries, were subject to British rule. The Realm reached its greatest size in 1928, and the phrase "The sun never sets on the British Empire" was coined. Most colonies and territories have now become part of the Commonwealth. See **Commonwealth** page 281.

SIR

A formal address for men who are Knights of the Realm, a title granted by the queen. "Sir" is always used with the full name and never with the surname alone.

Arise sir Marshall....

"If ever you find that you are to be presented to the Queen, do not rush up to her. She will be eventually brought round to you, like a dessert trolly at a good restaurant."
—*Los Angeles Times*

THE UNITED KINGDOM OF GREAT BRITAIN AND NORTHERN IRELAND

How to describe the component parts of the UK—and the group as a whole—is the source of great confusion for many Americans (and Brits, too). The UK consists of four countries: England, Northern Ireland, Scotland, and Wales. Are they separate countries? Well, yes and no. With the exception of England, each has its own parliament or assembly with certain powers and some degree of autonomy. Each country also elects representatives to the House of Commons in London. Geographically, England, Wales, and Scotland form a single island known as Great Britain. Northern Ireland, which lies across the Irish Sea, is part of the island of Ireland and is also part of the United Kingdom.

Confused yet? You will be, because there's also the term "British Isles," which refers not only to Great Britain and Northern Ireland, but also the rest of the island of Ireland (whose people have been known to resist inclusion), the Isle of Man, the Hebrides, the Shetland Islands, the Orkney Islands, the Isles of Scilly, and literally thousands of other small islands. The term does not, however, include the Channel Islands, which are self-governing Crown Dependencies.

> "I know why the sun never sets on the British Empire; God wouldn't trust an Englishman in the dark."
>
> —Duncan Spaeth

17.

Anatomy and Naughty Bits

EUPHEMISMS ARE MILD, INDIRECT, OR EVASIVE EXPRESSIONS that are used instead of words that might be offensive, unpleasant, or embarrassing. They are used by all societies in all areas of life but tend to be most common around perceived taboo areas, especially sex and bodily functions. The British and their emphasis on polite conversation are certainly no exception, and their somewhat unique set of "comfortable expressions" reveals a lot about their cultural values. It's more comfortable and less direct to say, "So sorry for your loss" rather than a rawer alternative like "Gorblimey, it's dreadful your mother got flattened under that lorry!"

Why do we replace perfectly normal words for perfectly normal body parts with nonsense sounds like "willy" and phrases like "front bottom"? What does that reveal about cultural attitudes toward sexuality and the body? Physical relations and bodily functions are laden with complicated societal, cultural, and pious baggage that inspires an endless stream of verbal evasion tactics.

Many euphemisms about sex and anatomy came about when it was considered extremely impolite to talk about such things.

You might think that euphemisms for private parts date back to the prudish Victorian era, and some do. But humans have used substitute words for thousands of years, as evidenced by euphemisms found in ancient Latin and Greek.

At the moment, many of us seem to be much less squeamish, and we're comparatively relaxed in speaking about sex and bodily functions. But be forewarned! Some entries that follow are neither "PG" nor "PC" and could cause offense.

ARSE

Ass or butt. "Don't be such a pain in the arse!"

ARSEHOLE

Asshole or contemptible person. Slang for the anus.

BOLLOCKS

Its literal meaning is, of course, testicles, but it can be used as a general term for nonsense ("What a load of bollocks"), a term of criticism ("That film was bollocks"), to call out a falsehood ("Alex is talking bollocks") or as a form of self-reproach ("Oh, bollocks, I've spilt the tea"). Despite its many uses, "bollocks" is essentially a swear word, albeit a relatively mild one. As with most things to do with body parts, the British have a plethora of euphemisms for testicles, including:

– Crown jewels   – Nuts
– Private parts   – Gonads (Nads)

- Goolies
- Cobblers
- Plums
- Knackers

- Goonies
- Hangings
- Nadgers

BEAKY

Nosy. The word "beak" is slang for a person's nose.

BELLOWS

Slang for the lungs.

BREAK WIND

To fart.

BUFF

Sexually attractive
- A word for nude, as in "She was in the buff!"
- Sometimes used loosely to describe the act of sex, e.g., "We was buffin' for hours."

BUGGERY

The act of anal sex.

BUM CLEAVAGE

Butt crack.

BUM

Butt. A person's bottom or rear end.

BUNCH OF FIVES

A fist, used in "I'll give you a bunch of fives!"

> "Continental people have sex lives; the English have hot water bottles."
>
> —George Mikes

CAKE HOLE

A person's mouth. "Shut yer cake hole!" See **Gob** page 293.

CHAT UP

To speak flirtatiously or "hit on" someone.

CHUNDER

To vomit or throw up. "That smell makes me want to chunder!" (This term originated in Australia.)

FANNY

Vagina. Not for use in polite conversation.
- Front bottom
- Quim
- Pranny

FIT

Attractive or sexy. (Not necessarily physically fit.)

GAGGING

Having a strong desire for something, usually sex. "She was gagging for it."

GET OFF

To kiss or make out with someone. Not, as in the USA, to have an orgasm.

GNASHERS

Teeth.

GOB

Mouth. Also saliva or phlegm.

JAP'S EYE

The penile opening.

JUBBLIES

Women's breasts. Here a few more terms:
- Baps—See **Bread roll** page 133.
- Belisha beacons
- Love blobs
- Love bubbles
- Strawberry creams
- Thrupney bits—Cockney rhyming slang for a woman's breasts (tits).
- Whammers

JUG HANDLES

Large and prominent ears.

KERB CRAWLER
A person who solicits street prostitutes.

KISSING TACKLE
Mouth and lips.

KNOB
Male genitalia. Here are a few more from a seemingly endless list:

- Dangly bits
- Hampton (Hackney) wick
- Lance
- Love muscle
- John Thomas
- Meat and two veg
- Naughty bits
- Organ
- Ovary tickler
- Pud
- Putz
- Rifle
- Todger
- Wedding tackle
- Wick

LAUGHING GEAR
Mouth.

LEAD IN ONE'S PENCIL
Male virility.

LEG OVER
Sexual intercourse. A few more:

- Bonk, as in "Fancy a bonk?"
- Get your end away
- Get stuffed

- Have it away
- Horizontal dancing
- Roger
- Rumpo
- Shag
- Slip it to someone

LUGHOLES

Ears. Derived from the Cockney rhyming slang term "Toby Jugs" (lugs).

ON THE PULL

Out looking for sex.

POO

Excrement. Usually a child's term, as in "Mummy, I need a poo." Also used as a verb as in "I'm going for a poo." Also "I'm in the poo now!" meaning "I'm in deep shit!"

PUDDING CLUB

"In the pudding club" means to be pregnant.

"Did I sleep with her? Not a wink, Reverend Father, not a wink."
—Brendan Behan

RANDY

"HI I'M RANDY!"

Horny, eager to engage in sex.
Americans named Randolph
should not introduce themselves
in British circles by saying "Hi,
I'm Randy," unless, of course....

RUDE BITS

Breasts and genitals.

RUMPY-PUMPY

Casual sex, used in a humorous way.

SLAP AND TICKLE

An informal, jokey expression meaning sexual play, possibly
including the full act but more often used to describe
lighthearted foreplay.

SLASH (LASH)

To urinate.

SNOG

Passionate kissing.

SPEND A PENNY

A polite euphemism for using the toilet, as in "Does anyone
need to spend a penny before we set off?" The term comes
from the cost of using a public toilet back in the day.

SPUNK

Sperm, semen. So, saying, "He/she's a real fighter, full of spunk" or "I'm a spunky guy" evokes great hilarity.

> "A friend of mine has the unfortunate job of handling complaints from customers. She had not long arrived from America when a particularly difficult customer came to see her in her office. After 40 minutes of sometimes insistent conversation, they emerged. She shook his hand and once he had gone, she turned to the other office workers and said "'Man! He was full of spunk.'"
>
> —Jenny Carruthers

STOCKING FILLERS

Female legs.

TICKER

Heart. Often used with the word "dicky" to indicate a bad heart. "He died of a dicky ticker."

TOBY JUG

Cockney rhyming slang for ears (lugs).

TOUCH UP

To molest sexually.

TROTTERS

Feet.

UP THE DUFF

To be pregnant.

WANK

To masturbate.

WANKER

Masturbator. Often shouted in traffic and usually accompanied by rude hand gestures.

WEE

A child's term for pee.

WILLIE-WELLIE

Condom. Here are a few more terms:

- French letter
- Rubber boot
- Raincoat
- Rubber Johnny
- Johnny

WILLY

Penis, often used by children. See **Knob** page 294.

"I was reading a book in school with a five-year-old. It was about the Tower of London and referred to the Crown Jewels. I asked her if she knew what the Crown Jewels were, and she said yes. If her dad got hit by a football accidentally, he'd say: 'Ow, mind my crown jewels!' (She said this complete with actions.)"

—Beverly Mackay

18.

Rhyming Slang

RHYMING SLANG IS A MYSTERIOUS PHENOMENON THAT developed simultaneously in large urban areas all over the country during the late 1800s. The most well-known is Cockney rhyming slang, which took root in the East End of London, but there are also versions from Manchester, Glasgow, Birmingham, and even Dorset. In rhyming slang, a word is replaced with a different word or phrase that rhymes with it, e.g., "feet" becomes "plates of meat," and "stairs" becomes "apple and pears." I've heard that the original purpose was to throw off the police and tax collectors. For the uninitiated, Cockney rhyming slang can be pretty confusing. Don't try speaking it if you don't know all the ins and outs.

Here are just a few Cockney rhyming slang phrases to get you started.

- Adam and Eve = Believe "Would you Adam and Eve it?"
- Apples and Pears = Stairs
- Ayrton Senna or Cock and hen = £10
- Bag of sand = One thousand pounds (grand)

- Boat race = Face, as in "Nice legs, shame about the boat race."
- Board and plank = an American (Yank)
- Barnet Fair = Hair "Don't touch me Barnet, I've just had it done."
- Barney Rubble = Trouble, as in "They had a bit of a barney."
- Bottle = Bravery/bravado, in reference to a boxer. "He's got a lot of bottle," or conversely, "He lost his bottle."
- Bottle and Glass = Ass
- Brahms and Liszt = Pissed (drunk), as in "Sorry, I was a bit Brahms and Liszt last night."
- Bricks and Mortar = Daughter
- Bubble (bubble and squeak) = Greek
- Butcher's (butcher's hook) = Look, as in "Give us a butcher's at your new watch."
- China (china plate) = Mate, as in "You alright, me old China?"
- Cream crackered (knackered) = Exhausted, worn out
- Currant bun = Sun
- Deep sea diver = £5 (fiver)
- Dog and bone = Phone, as in "Call me on the dog and bone."
- Dustbin Lid = Kid, a child.
- Hackney Marshes (glasses) = Spectacles, binoculars
- Half inch (pinch) = Steal, as in "He half inched that watch."
- Hampton Wick (prick, dick) = Penis.
- Jam jar = Car

Rhyming Slang.

- Jimmy Riddle (piddle) = Urinate (piddle)
- Khyber Pass = Arse
- Lady Godiva = £5 (fiver)
- Lager and lime = Time
- Lemon squeezer (geezer) = Man
- Lemon squeezy = Easy, as in "Easy peasy, lemon squeezy."
- Leo Sayer (dayer) = All day
- Loaf (bread) = Head, as in "Use your loaf!"
- Locker = Memory (knocker = head)
- Lone Ranger = Danger
- Mince pies = Eyes

- Nat King Cole (dole) = Unemployed (on the dole)
- Navigator = Potato
- Needle and thread = Bread
- Nelson Mandela = Stella Artois lager
- Northants = Underpants
- Not on yer nellie = "Not on your life," a shortened version of "Nelly Duff." Nelly Duff = puff (breath)
- Oxo cube (Tube) = London Underground
- Paraffin = Gin
- Pete Toing = Wrong
- Pogo stick (prick, dick) = Penis
- Polo mint (skint) = Penniless
- Pony and trap = Crap, as in "I'm off for a pony."
- Pop goes the weasel = Diesel
- Porkies pies (pork pies) = Lies, as in "She's telling porkies."
- Posh and becks (sex) = Sexual intercourse
- Postman's knock = Clock
- Prawn crackers (knackers) = Testicles
- Quaker oat = Coat
- Ramsgate Sands = Hands
- Red rum (dumb) = Quiet, timid
- Rhythm and blues = Shoes
- Riddle-me-ree (pee) = Urinate
- Ringo Starr = Car
- Rip Van Winkle (tinkle) = Urinate
- Roger Moore = Snore
- Rosie Lea = Tea, as in "Let's have nice cup of Rosie Lea."
- Rosie O'Grady = Lady

- Sailors at sea = Tea
- Sally Gunnell = Tunnel, particularly London's Blackwall Tunnel
- Samuel Pepys (creeps) = Feeling of unease
- Scarborough Fair = Hair
- Scooby Doo = Clue, as in "Sorry, I haven't got a Scooby."
- Septic (septic tank) = Yank / American
- Sherbert dab (cab) = Taxi
- Sherbert dip (tip) = Gratuity
- Smack in the eye = Pie
- Stan and Ollie (brollie) = Umbrella
- Struggle and strife = Life
- Sweaty (socks) = Jocks / Scottish
- Syrup (of fig) = Wig
- Tea leaf = Thief, as in "He's a tea leaf."
- Tom Tit = Shit, as in "Just off for a Tom Tit."
- Trilby hat (prat) = Fool
- Trouble and strife = Wife
- Whistle and flute = Suit, as in "Nice whistle you've got on today."

19.

Bits and Bobs

I'M OFTEN IMPRESSED WITH HOW MANY TERMS AND CONCEPTS defy classification. As humans, we like to label and categorize everything in an attempt to understand and exercise an element of control over it. This is certainly true in the areas of relationships, science, politics, and geography, to name but a few. However, try as we might, not everything will fit neatly into a predetermined pigeonhole. When we come across an item that resists a label, we set it aside in the hope that inspiration will provide an answer someday and allow us to assign a proper place in our catalogue of life. Of course, this seldom happens. As life goes on, we find ourselves with an ever-expanding collection of metaphysical "bits and bobs."

Nowhere is this phenomenon more evident than in the area of linguistics. Language is constantly growing and evolving. As new words and terms enter the vernacular, and old ones leave, a little chaos inevitably results. Enjoy these terms that don't quite fit in any other category.

BANK HOLIDAY

I was always curious as to why several of the holidays in the UK are called "bank holidays," and I've never received a credible answer as to why the banks take a day off several times a year. The most widespread explanation is that the banks use that time to catch up on their bookkeeping. This seems to be reason enough for the entire country to shut down, and these days have become standard holiday days for Britain. The bank holidays in Britain are:

- New Year's Day
- Good Friday
- Easter Monday
- Early May Bank Holiday
- Late May Bank Holiday. Usually coincides with Memorial Day in the USA.
- August Bank Holiday
- Christmas Day
- Boxing Day (the day after Christmas)

Any time a bank holiday falls on a weekend, the day off is moved to the following Monday. On bank holidays, the visitor can expect that motorways will be very busy, hotel rooms will be more difficult to book or will be more expensive, children will be out of school, and family attractions will be noticeable busier.

BANK NOTE

Also known as a "currency bill" or "legal tender." Some bank notes in the UK are printed on polymer, which is a thin and flexible plastic material, and some are printed on paper. The paper notes are gradually being phased out. While there are four denominations of bank notes in England, Scotland and North Ireland also print bank notes. Those issued in England are

- £5—featuring Sir Winston Churchill, polymer
- £10—featuring the author Jane Austen, polymer
- £20—featuring the economist Adam Smith, paper
- £20—featuring the artist JMW Turner, polymer
- £50—featuring the inventors Mathew Boulton and James Watt, paper
- £50—featuring the mathematician Alan Turing, polymer

The £1 note was withdrawn from circulation in 1988 and replaced with a coin. Some retailers outside of Scotland and North Ireland refuse to accept the bank notes issued in those jurisdictions.

BOULES

A French game played extensively in England in which metal balls are thrown so that they land as close as possible to a smaller ball, called the "jack." Similar to the Italian game of bocce, it is also known as "bowls" in the UK. (Pronounced "bools.")

"In England, if you commit a crime, the police don't have a gun, and you don't have a gun. If you commit a crime, the police will say, 'Stop, or I'll say, stop again!'"

—Robin Williams

COUNTY SHOW

County fair. A shire's agricultural fair with farm animals, vegetable displays, and baking contests.

CRICKET

A bat-and-ball game. It has become ingrained in English culture and folklore and has come to represent the nostalgic and gentle side of country life. Its connection with fair play is so strong that the name of the game has come to be used for propriety itself. You will often hear the phrase, "Well, it's just not cricket, is it?"

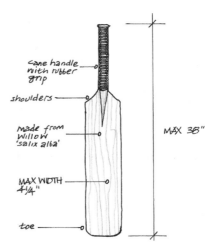

"The English are not a very spiritual people, so they invented cricket to give them some idea of eternity."

—George Bernard Shaw

DAILIES

> Newspapers appearing each day or each weekday. May also refer to a person employed to do cleaning or other household work by the day.

FLORIN

> A former British coin, originally made of silver and later cupronickel, a copper-nickel alloy. Equivalent to ten (new) pence, it was discontinued in 1971.

"In 1993, I decided to take a trip to Stratford-upon-Avon to see Shakespeare territory and attend a couple of plays at the new theatre there. There were no direct trains and I had to change at one point—I can't remember where. The old-fashioned transfer station had an ancient tearoom. I had a 45-minute wait, so I decided to investigate. I opened the door to find two older ladies in aprons and strange-looking bonnets standing behind the counter and sizing me up. The place was empty except for the three of us. I tentatively approached the counter and asked for a cup of tea. It came with milk and sugar in a cracked cup, even though I don't take sugar. I asked how much it was, and the attendant said, 'That'll be a florin, love.' Having no idea what a florin looked like, I reached into my pocket and pulled out all my change. I held it out to her like a small child. Both attendants burst into laughter, and one said, 'You can have the tea, dear. That's the best laugh we've had in a long time.'"

—Joseph Houghton

HIGHLAND COW

A breed of cattle that must be seen to be believed. They have very long, shaggy red hair to help them cope with the quite harsh Scottish winters. Their long horns make them an instantly recognizable icon of Highland Scotland. There are claims that they are the oldest cattle breed in the world.

HOGMANAY

The New Year's Eve celebration traditionally observed in Scottish homes. It is filled with symbolic acts such as the bringing of the coal. May involve haggis; always involves whisky.

My first experience of a Scottish New Year celebration was in 1988, when a group of friends and I traveled there. As we approached Berwick-upon-Tweed, just south of the border on the eastern side of the country, the driver of the car pulled off to the side of the road, and everyone proceeded to pull out their passports and some Scottish five-pound notes. "Where's your passport?" they asked and then enquired whether I'd changed any money. When I explained that I didn't know that any of this was necessary, they scowled at me for a moment. Then, unable to contain themselves, they burst into laughter at my expense. It was a great start to a great New Year's celebration.

—M.H.

KNACKER'S YARD

The place to which horse carcasses (or old, injured, or dying beasts) were removed to be rendered down to fats, bone, and soap. Now an expression of exhaustion or frailty, as in "I'm fit only for the knacker's yard."

MARKET DAY

Many towns in Britain have a designated day of the week when their outdoor market is held. Market stalls may sell fruit and vegetables, flowers, meat, and fish. Local organizations and charity shops also sponsor booths.

PENNY

The smallest-value coin, analogous to the American penny. The plural is "pence."

RAF

Royal Air Force.

ROUNDERS

A British game similar to baseball but not identical. If you're a baseball fan, this game will only upset you.

RSJ

A "Rolled steel joist" (also known as "I-beam"), used in construction. (Not to be confused with the Religious Sisters of St Joseph, a religious order with communities in Australia, New Zealand, Ireland, and South America!)

SAS

The Special Air Service, used for commando, covert, or assault assignments. Together with the SBS (Special Boat Service), they form the UK's Special Forces, the equivalent of which in the USA would be the Navy SEALs and the Army Special Forces (Green Berets).

SHILLING

An old British coin, roughly comparable to an American nickel. Twenty shillings were equal to one pound. The shilling was a small, silver-colored coin that was used from the 1500s until Britain decimalized its currency in 1971. Although they were discontinued in 1966, shillings remained legal tender until 1990, with a value of five new pence. The popular nickname for a shilling was a "bob."

THRUPPENCE

A twelve-sided coin, worth three old pence, that became obsolete in 1971. The term remains in occasional use as rhyming slang for "tits": "thruppenny bits."

V-SIGN

A hand gesture made with a raised index and middle finger. Made palm-forward, it is universally recognizable as a Churchillian "V for Victory" and a 1960s peace sign, and it is still popular on social media. Turn the hand around, however, and it becomes a British sign meaning "Fuck off," as clearly understood as the North American middle finger. Why two fingers? According to folklore, its usage dates back to the Battle of Agincourt. So deadly were the English archers that, if captured, the two fingers they used to pull back the bowstring would be chopped off by the French. The English would therefore taunt their foes by displaying these fingers. True or not, it's a good story!

WATER BOATMAN

A water insect with oar-like back legs that propel it through the water.

WOODBINES

A very old British brand of strong and unfiltered cigarettes. They were used extensively during World War I and are well known but not popular today.

Afterword

E NGLAND WAS FOR CENTURIES A CELTIC ISLAND WHOSE inhabitants spoke a collection of Brittonic languages until 43 CE, when the Romans invaded. They imposed their language, resulting in a Celtic-Latin hybrid. In the fifth century, the Romans left, and the Germanic tribes filled the void, adding Germanic tribal tongues to what was quickly becoming English. Then, in the eighth century, the Vikings began raiding neighboring northeast England. Eventually, the Danes decided to settle permanently in England. They were assimilated into the English population, adding the Danish language to the mix. The Norman Conquest of England in 1066 initiated ongoing Norman French influence, resulting in French becoming the lingua franca of the royal court and government in England. Today, there are nearly ten thousand French words in modern English. In the sixteenth century, the English embarked on empire-building of their own, imposing their language on the rest of the world and simultaneously absorbing words from the colonies into English.

Within this brief linguistic history of English is a testimony to its elasticity, its ability to absorb and amend new words and phrases from outside and within, and to make them its own. Over

315

the centuries, English has evolved and adapted readily to social and cultural changes.

The result is that this guide will have a limited life. The British English defined here will morph in ways impossible to predict. In researching this work, I have come across numerous examples of lovely and quaint colloquialisms that have died from lack of use. I have also discovered brand-new sayings, words, and phrases in current English, many the result of external influences. Homogenization, both within the UK and trans-Atlantic, has been accelerated in recent decades by globalization, technology, social media, and ever-increasing American influence on Britain, its culture, and its language.

As I researched words, phrases, histories, and pronunciations, I began to realize how much of the rich colloquial history of Britain has already been lost. The inexorable shrinking of the world and the diminished power of geography is moving both Brits and Yanks toward a monoculture and a homogeneous language.

You will, of course, recognize that considering the patchwork quilt that is British English, there are a number of words and phrases that have been left out of this guide. Others have multiple definitions, not all of which are included here. I hope this is at least a good place to start, and that you find this collection to be useful and entertaining.

I'm off for a kip! Blimey, I'm knackered!

Acknowledgments

THE AUTHOR WOULD LIKE TO ACKNOWLEDGE THE MANY contributions of stories, words and phrases made by friends and colleagues. Specific debts of gratitude must be acknowledged to Beverly Mackay who performed the initial proofreading, Mark Cowie who created the illustrations, and to Marion Townsend who coordinated the illustrations.

I would also like to acknowledge the three editors who toiled countless hours getting this manuscript into the current state: Peter Thody, David Johnstone, and Tom Herbertson. The collaboration with Peter, David and Tom have greatly increased the breadth, detail, and total number of terms defined in this book. And appreciation to Sue Campbell for the book design.

A special acknowledgment to Mark Sedenquist and Megan Edwards of Imbrifex Books whose experience and guidance have made this book possible.

About the Author

A PROFESSOR OF SOCIO-ANTHROPOLOGY WITH A LIFELONG interest in travel and linguistics, Marshall Hall began life on an Ohio farm. He moved from the University of Cincinnati to teach at the American College in London. Thirty-three years later, he still calls the UK home. He is married to an English woman, has UK citizenship, and lives in Chesham, Buckinghamshire, just outside central London.

Connect with the author online:

f @MarshallHallAuthor

O @MarshallHall15

Index

H

I

L

M

Wren, Christopher 254
wurzel 92

Y
Yank 218
yard 22
yew 184
Y-fronts 241
yob (yobbo) 92
yonks 78
Yorkies 217
York, Peter 38
Yorkshire 184
Yorkshire pudding 164. *See*
 also Sunday roast
Young, Lester 238

Z
Zebedee 218
zebra crossing 114
zed 54
zones 268